WHAT LEADERSHIP IS FOR

IDENTIFYING THE THREE DRIVERS FOR STAND-OUT PERFORMANCE

'An inspiring and modern way to see leadership.'
Jaime de Pinies, former lead economist, World Bank and former head of research, Santander Investment

'There's an important place for management theory, but nothing quite beats the practical experience coming from those who've faced both the everyday and the longer term challenges of leadership.'
James Capon, former president, Levi's Brand and president, Dockers

'A clear and insightful perspective on what leadership should be today.'
Dr Constance Cramer, Aspen Institute Fellow, former deputy director, Global Health Initiative, Boston University.

'In Africa, leadership is a very hot topic, becoming more and more complex. Faniel's model shares some great insights and keys to unlock performance and lead effectively in the everchanging world of work.'
Emily Kamunde-Osoro, leadership coach and founder of East African HR Symposium.

'In today's VUCA world, business leaders need a strong compass. Having this compass will boost engagement and performance within the entire organization.'
Dr Martin Emrich, leadership expert, bestselling author of Leading in a VUCA World

THE AUTHOR

Patrick Faniel is managing director of Management Centre Europe (MCE), a leading force in developing and inspiring leaders and managers in Europe, the Middle East and Africa.

As part of the American Management Association, MCE runs open programmes and customized learning solutions for executives, teams and organizations, bringing them up to speed with how they can become more efficient, more agile and more attractive to the next generation of talent.

As a chief executive, as a founder, as a professor and in business development, Patrick Faniel has been transforming performance in ventures of all sizes for the last 25 years. At MCE, he now leads a team and an international faculty with direct strategic and operational experience of the complex challenges that leaders are now facing.

WHAT LEADERSHIP IS FOR

IDENTIFYING THE THREE DRIVERS
FOR STAND-OUT PERFORMANCE

PATRICK FANIEL

NOVARO
PUBLISHING

What Leadership is For: Identifying three drivers for stand-out performance

Every possible effort has been made to ensure that the information contained in this publication is accurate at the time of going to press. Neither the publisher nor the authors can accept responsibility for any errors or omissions, however caused. Nor can any responsibility be accepted for loss or damage as a result of reading this publication.

Published by Novaro Publishing Ltd, 2 Speedwell Drive, Lindfield, West Sussex
e: publish@novaropublishing.com.

ISBN: 978-1-7398640-6-4
E-ISBN: 978-1-7398640-7-1

A CIP catalogue record for this book is available from the British Library.

Designed by Chantel Barnett, Clear Design CC Ltd

For further details about our titles and our authors, see:
www.novaropublishing.com

To my wife, Johanne

'You never fail until you stop trying.'
Albert Einstein

'Effective leadership is not about making speeches or being liked;
leadership is defined by results not attributes.'
Peter Drucker

CONTENTS

INTRODUCTION

In our rapidly changing world, where a breakthrough innovation or an external crisis can shake up an industry completely from one day to the next, leadership has become extremely complex. To lead organizations, teams or people is not only a question of style nor one of agility, the buzz word. Leadership demands a combination of skills, competencies and choices to drive a strategy forward in a specific direction with clear goals and focus. Try to do it all and you will be caught in the middle, pulled in too many directions.

We instinctively recognise the distinctive drive of charismatic leaders like Jack Welch at GE, Bill Gates at Microsoft, Elon Musk at Tesla and SpaceX, Steve Jobs at Apple, Richard Branson at Virgin and Bernard Arnaud at LVMH. Leadership, we all agree, is about driving an organization and leading teams. Leadership, yes, but what for?

What is driving you as a leader and what are you trying to cascade through your organization? Leadership has to have a clear focus to be efficient. Without it, you don't know where to go, you can't inspire teams and you can't boost performance, and you can't optimize the competencies required to achieve your goals.

When you observe widely known, high-performing companies, when you read what their leaders write and say, you will notice they always focus on maybe one, two or three clearly identified areas, so giving a clear sense of direction to their organization and their teams. They know what their leadership is for.

This book will present a model that allows leaders to choose the direction they want to take for themselves and the organization they represent. It will explain each of twelve possible areas where they can focus to bring value. As a leader, you are responsible for all of them. For stand-out performance, however, you will give priority to three at most. The remaining areas must continue to be there, of course, but in the background. As you will see, some combinations are ideal and bring more value.

It is part of your role to make choices. What is your leadership for? You will dedicate 75 percent of your time, energy and effort to those three areas, fully aligning your organization to how follow-up actions are taken, whether it is in how you communicate or how you recruit. Alignment is key.

It is obvious that leaders operate first to make a profit and/or benefit society. Many organizations strive to do both. Depending on their goals, the cursor points more towards making a profit or contributing to society. But nowadays both are present.

More and more, there is pressure to benefit society. It doesn't exclude making a profit, of course. The position of the cursor will determine how far a leader wants to go, giving direction to the organization when making decisions and implementing plans. It is the backdrop to the twelve drivers we are going to explore, which is where leaders can create real value.

Without a clear choice of which three to pursue and without aligning the organization, however, your efficiency as a leader will diminish and tensions between competing priorities will result in non-performance, as well as other consequences, such as losing talent or lack of engagement.

Profit focus   **Social focus**

Figure 1: the ultimate driver, a subtle combination of making profits and positive social impact

In the following pages, we are first going to explore further the concept of this book. We will then review each of the twelve drivers of value split into four parts: business, process, people and market. In each chapter, we hear from a well-known company about why their leaders are choosing to focus on that driver. They will explain how they do it, how they see leadership and what leadership means for their organization.

In Part 1, Business, we will address leadership for growth, innovation and partnerships. In Part 2, Process, we will go through leadership for strategy execution, effectiveness and digitalization. In Part 3, People, we analyse employee experience, diversity and inclusion, and inspiration. Finally, in Part 4, Market, we will discuss leadership for customer focus, for branding and for personalization. Before the conclusion, you will also find an additional chapter on leadership without authority, as so many are now finding themselves being asked to lead outside conventional lines of hierarchy and control.

By the end, I hope that you won't see companies and their leaders in the same way. You will be able to identify what drives them. Before making your own choices for your organization, you will understand what their leadership is for. In its design, this book gives you a guide to each of these drivers, helping you to select and implement the right ones for your organization. There is no best choice. There is only a choice that will be clear to all in taking your organization forward.

1.

CONCEPT

What is key for leaders is to decide with their stakeholders where to put their focus, energy and efforts: what their leadership is for. Depending on the environment, the competitors, the constraints, the expectations of stakeholders, the optimization of results, the resources, the talents and the structure, that focus can vary significantly.

In some companies, charisma will be what matters most, but only for certain personalities and in particular environments. If the leader is charismatic, perhaps it might be best to play that card to the full. If, instead, the environment is highly competitive, it might be better to concentrate first on rapid innovation. If talent determines performance, a focus on employee experience will probably bring the best results.

Through our work as a leading global provider of management development at Management Centre Europe (mce.eu), we have identified twelve potential drivers, which can be split into four quadrants. Each of them must be taken into account in how you operate a team, but a choice can be made about which really drive the organization. Hence our model: what leadership is for.

As a leader, you need to manage those twelve areas, but not equally. Part of your role is to make a choice, selecting a maximum of three areas. You will then dedicate 75 percent of your time, energy and efforts to those, fully aligned to how you act as a company.

A company focused on innovation but unable to keep its talents or unable to listen to the market will, of course, fail. Our point here is to make sure leadership is putting more efforts into a couple of areas, where it can outperform and where the direction is clear to everybody.

No judgment is being made about which is good or bad. It depends on you. It is not because a company focuses on internal processes, not on employees, that it is underperforming: perhaps it is the right choice for that company. No judgment. We can have an opinion and feel frustrated by a company overlooking the market and the expectations of its customers, but it doesn't make it wrong. It is about making clear choices. Our model is there to understand, to implement and to outperform.

Quadrant 1: Business

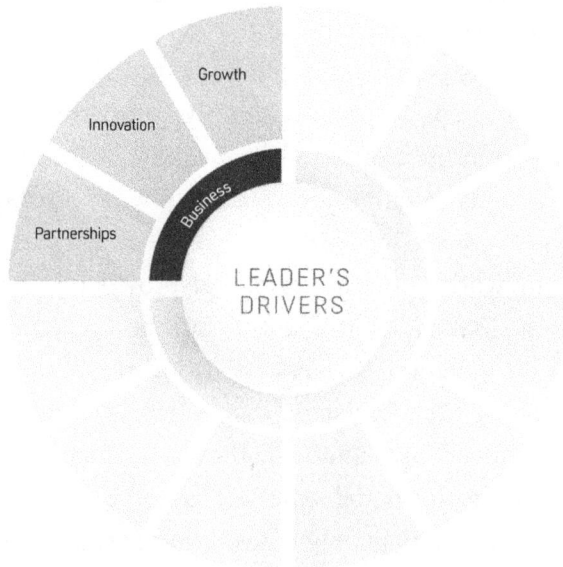

The first three areas are linked to the business: the focus can be put on growth, on innovation or on partnerships to increase value. Leaders who choose one of those drivers will manage teams differently.

Leading a company for growth requires specific leadership: pushing for revenue and/or for acquisitions (with the challenges of integration and alignment). How do you get teams focused and hungry for sales and for growth? Most organizations are seeking sales, but growth is a different story. If growth is the driver, the focus has to find expression in any messages, rewards, structures, processes and recruits for your teams.

When speaking about innovation, we distinguish between breakthroughs and a more structured process. If somebody suddenly has a brilliant idea that changes the rules, it is one thing. You cannot allow for it or base your future on it happening. As a leader with innovation as a driver, how do you build a culture in an organization and lead for innovation? The traditional way is to have a head of innovation, driving the initiatives and research. For that, many models exist. This is how the Covid vaccine was developed.

But in our world, innovation can be driven by any employee, by clients, by suppliers and so can come from anywhere in the company. Leadership encourages the creation and deployment of such value.

The third possibility for business is leadership for partnerships. Some leaders understand that performance relies on putting strong partnerships and alliances in place. They benefit from strategic collaborations to realise stronger, more sustainable value together, as well as building a competitive advantage for themselves. Such leaders are driving their organization differently from those that are internally controlled.

Quadrant 2: Process

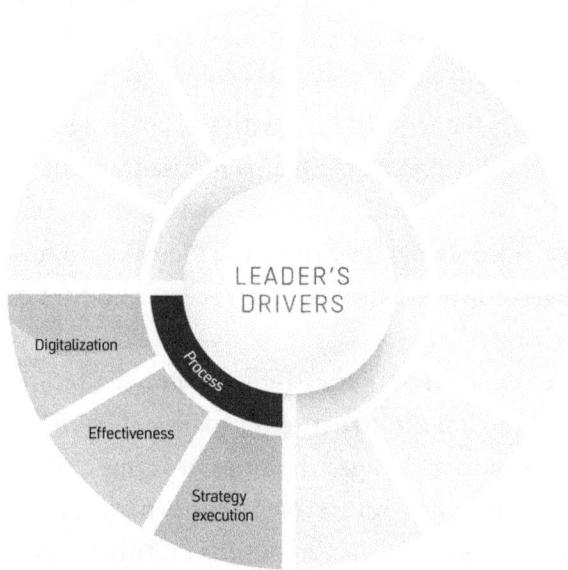

Some companies will decide to focus on their processes to achieve success. This quadrant is then more about internal focus, which has an impact on the value proposition and clients, but the internal alignment on ways to act and operate is primary.

Let's take the first driver, strategy execution. A lot of strategies fail, not because they are faulty, but through lack of execution. Implementing a strategy is not about communicating it. Instead, it is a structured process, where consequences are aligned in various areas. Leadership for strategy execution is then about making sure that people understand what the strategy means for them and about aligning processes on the objective. It is no easy task. If leaders know implementation is key to realising outstanding results for a strategy, then the driver lies here. At MCE we have often observed, it combines as a driver with one from the market quadrant to create a really winning pair.

Recent work at Antwerpen University has defined leadership for our times as getting things done. Leadership for effectiveness is about driving any action in the organization for results, finding the right leaders with the right competencies in all areas of action.

In process, the last driver is digitalization. It's not just about how you connect to the market, but as a real transformation, from inside, into a digital company. This type of change is not only about technology or data. It relies heavily on people. It is a complete redesign of the organization, based on digital.

So leadership for digital impact is not about selling through the internet. It is about transforming an organization to the point that digital is everywhere: starting from the strategy through to the way people are recruited, how they work and the customer experience.

Quadrant 3: People

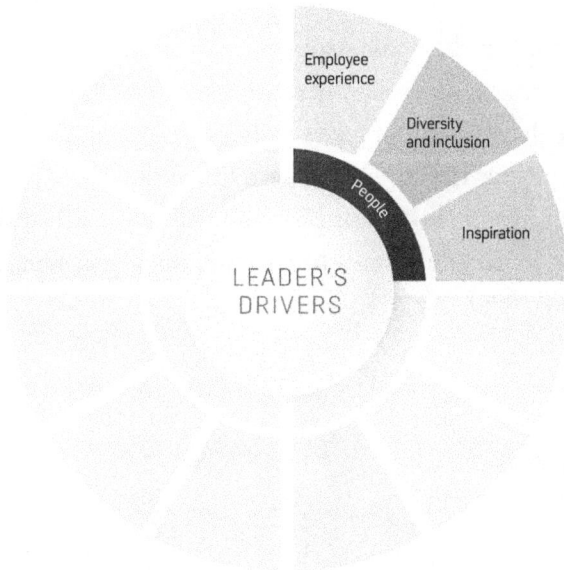

Employee experience

Diversity and inclusion

People

Inspiration

LEADER'S DRIVERS

Organizations depend on talent. How many authors speak nowadays about the war for talent, engagement and how to attract the best employees? If people are the real drivers of an organization, leaders have three choices about where to focus.

First is what we call the employee experience. It's about more than checking levels of engagement. It's about the fundamentals of managing the whole experience of employees with you, creating a sustainable framework that gives you the flexibility and depth to transform the workplace, while keeping and attracting the best talent. It's about creating an experience similar to securing the loyalty of customers.

Going further into diversity, equity, inclusion and belonging (DEIB) can give companies a distinct advantage. Research tells us that it is creating better solutions and opening up more talent. However, it is significantly more than what the law demands. Instead, it has to be a definite choice, a conviction, which focuses on diversity to expand the potential.

As discussed earlier, charisma is a powerful driver in its own right. However, it is a rare quality and cannot be taught. Inspiration is something else: the leader leads by inspiring others. Pushing others to follow. Whatever the direction, people feel the passion. We are here in the domain of soft skills, soft power. If this is the driver, leaders will design ways to cascade stories to their teams about what makes the organization special.

Quadrant 4: Market

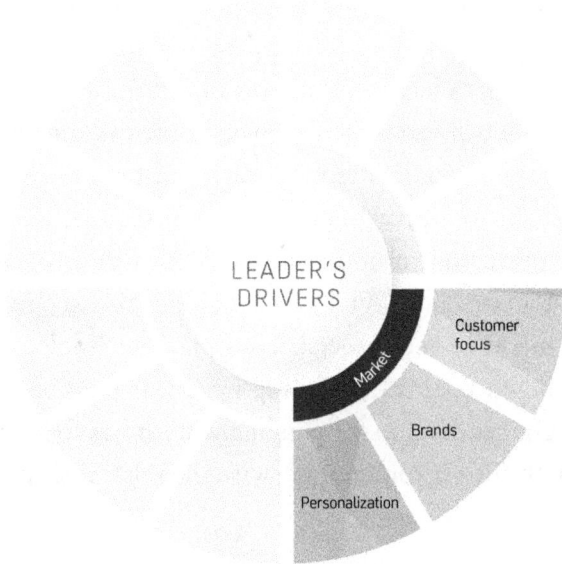

The last quadrant is about concentrating outside on clients and on the market. Drivers come from outside. It is a difficult focus to have, especially when trying to translate it into behaviours throughout the company. Customers set the tone. They live the experience with you, good or bad, then speak about it.

In the first driver in this quadrant, leadership turns everyone's attention to customers in all they do. It is easy to say you are putting your customers first. In fact, it is much harder for leaders to overcome a culture dominated by hard financial figures and match it with customer insights around which teams can organize. You might even be making profits without taking your customers into account. Such leaders realise such a position is unsustainable in the longer term. Instead, they design the whole company around the experience it is giving customers, touchpoint by touchpoint.

The second driver puts all efforts into the brand and what it represents. For those leaders, who can ingrain a brand's vision into how an organization behaves and how it reaches its publics, it can be the most powerful way of future proofing a business. However, it depends on having a clear sense of how brands now compete as value disciplines. There is no room to compete in the middle anymore.

Finally, the personalization of each customer's experience is influencing performance in more and more sectors. Each customer has the perception that products and services are uniquely tailored for them. Of course, a factory sits behind the scenes, but each customer is made to feel special. Nowadays technology, especially artificial intelligence, is transforming what it is possible to offer, but it is not enough. Leadership for personalization has to happen at each touchpoint with the customer, otherwise the relationship falters.

Conclusion

Putting all the quadrants together gives you a full picture of the model and all the potential drivers for leaders. Now that we have identified all twelve, let's explore each of them in more detail.

Once a focus is chosen, leadership is about finding a way to drive the organization and teams forward towards it. Alignment and cascades vary for each. Real value lies in mastering each of these challenges, then combining with one or two others. That is the way to stand-out performance.

PART 1

BUSINESS

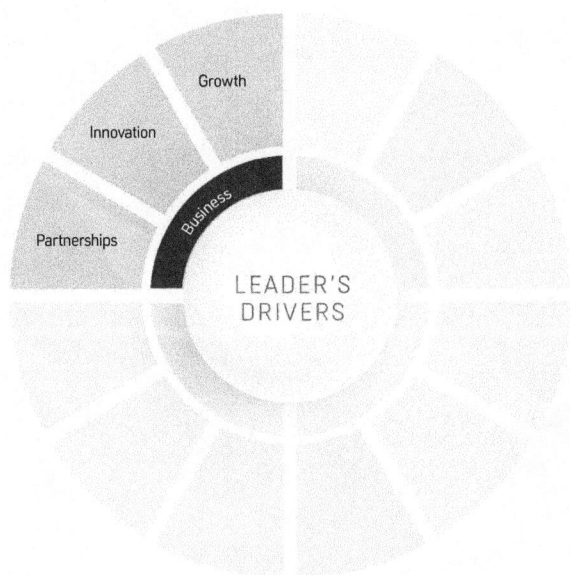

Growth

Innovation

Partnerships

Business

LEADER'S
DRIVERS

Growth

Employee experience

Diversity and inclusion

Innovation

Partnerships

Business

People

Inspiration

LEADER'S DRIVERS

Digitalization

Customer focus

Process

Market

Effectiveness

Brands

Strategy execution

Personalization

2.

LEADERSHIP FOR GROWTH

One idea takes you so far. Perhaps to a business of €1 million. What takes revenue up to €10 million, €100 million and beyond is the ability of leaders to create a compelling vision for how they are going to create value for their customers and build an organization that responds to their expectations and beliefs.

We see the difference that leaders can make most dramatically between those few start-ups that grow exponentially and the many who fail to lift off. A powerful idea is not enough, if you don't gain traction and find a repeating revenue model.

The underlying mistake that so many make, as Simon Sinek argues in his classic TED talk about Golden Circles, is to rely on the rational 'what' of their offer, instead of the power of its emotional 'why'. It's a rare gift to pitch to hopes and dreams. It's that appeal, however, that has allowed a company like Apple to keep re-inventing itself in different forms of media, instead of competing on its capabilities in technology or design.

At the level of a more traditional organization, the same principles open up the potential for trading at a premium and competing with the world's best. Such was the case for Russell Houghton, a member of the MCE faculty, who took part in the transformation of how value was created at the British engineer IMI, formerly Imperial Metal Industries.

For him, the path to getting ahead of the curve lies in first creating a vision and wiring your business with a strategy that put the right people, products and processes in place. 'It then all depends on a team of leaders who can deliver the growth.'

We all instinctively know such leaders. Their motives might vary, whether they are scaling for profit or aiming to become the winner who takes it all. Whatever metrics they follow, revenue growth is ultimately what drives them all.

In my first job, the chief executive analysed sales report every day, comparing performance week by week, month by month, year by year. Everyone knew what was expected and understood how they could contribute. Growth seemed to be the only thing that really mattered. The first discussions of the day were about this week's sales versus the year before. Client satisfaction was about growing the business. Technology was about convincing new clients. Partnerships were about expanding markets. PR was about winning new business.

At MCE, we often explore the potential for creating such a mindset for growth with organizations. Growth is their ultimate objective, of course, but how do their leaders actually go about translating that strategy into reality?

Growth mindsets

However much leaders aspire to growth, for many it remains elusive. In the 2010s, according to McKinsey & Co, the typical company grew at 2.8 percent a year, half the rate of the previous decade. Over a longer period, only one in ten of America's leading companies grew more than national income did over 30 years.

For those in the top quarter of growers in the first half of the 2010s, only a third repeated that performance in the second half of the decade. Growth, it seems, has a strong tendency to revert to the norm.

However, sustainable profitable growth is within reach, says McKinsey in its 2022 report, *Choosing to Grow*: 'When sustainable, inclusive, and profitable growth becomes a conscious, resolute choice, it shapes decision-making across every area of the business. Growth becomes the oxygen of an organization, feeding the culture, elevating ambitions and inspiring a sense of purpose. Growth leaders generate 80 percent more shareholder value than their peers over a ten-year period.'

So what are the mindsets of such growth leaders? In a 2019 report, McKinsey identified seven behaviours that separate them from the pack:

- I am all in.
- I am willing to fail.
- I know my customer as a person, not as a data point.
- I favour action over perfection.
- I fight for growth.
- I have a growth story I tell all the time.
- I give control to others.

McKinsey found that leaders who display more than 70 percent of these mindsets manage to grow their top line twice as fast as everyone else: 'growth is a journey that requires the entire business to constantly adjust, optimise and execute, but it starts at the top'.

Accelerated growth

What we assume about the speed of growth is changing too. We can no longer think in a gradual, linear way. Instead, ventures are now using technology to scale exponentially. That's why you might find yourself up against organizations that are ten times better, faster or cheaper than yours, argues Salim Ismail in his book, *Exponential Organizations* (2014).

Growth used to depend on incrementally adding to your assets, such as equipment or people. Information faces no such limitations. Instead, it can grow exponentially, doubling in size as it grows. Such growth is deceptive at first: 0.1 to 0.2 to 0.4, all look close to not much. However, such doublings soon add up to millions and billions.

Such exponential organizations are characterised by massive transformation purpose, expressed as big and audacious goals. For them, it is never just a question of technology, but something that captures the imagination. Operationally, they tend to:

- recruit skills on demand rather than rely on big internal teams;

- source ideas, feedback, validation and even funding through community and the crowd;

- deploy algorithms to process data and automate themselves;

- rent, lease or leverage assets, except those that are mission critical;

- engage with their ecosystems to create feedback loops and ripple effects.

As organizations, they adopt a lightweight structure, where the emphasis is on adaptability, rather than efficiency. Instead of a classic hierarchical structure, what matters is everyone being a self-starter with an entrepreneurial mindset.

Beyond the constraints of scale

Demand can be rising rapidly, even exponentially, and popularity may be soaring. However, only a few start-ups go on to become stable giants, according to an article in the *Harvard Business Review* (Jeffrey F. Rayport, Davide Sola and Martin Kemp, February 2023).

In the early stages, a venture explores what value it can offer customers before finding a 'product-market fit'. Then when it completes the cycle, it fine tunes its business model and sharpens its competitive advantage.

In the middle of the cycle, as demand rises, leaders strive to achieve a 'profit-market fit'. In this often overlooked scaling phase, leaders search for the secret to lasting, profitable growth: that point when each new customer brings in additional revenue while only incurring marginal cost.

By now the venture will have an ambitious target, such as a fivefold increase in revenue and a tenfold increase in operating margin. However, no chain is stronger than the weakest link. So through 'relentless experimentation', leaders will be seeking to remedy each constraint on growth in order of significance.

'After they have moved beyond the early stage,' says *HBR*, 'almost all growing ventures routinely need to re-invent themselves and refine their core business.'

At the stage of scaling a venture, leaders will be ambidextrous enough to mix strategic experiment with commercial discipline. Typically, they will rely on:

- being modular, distributing authority to teams, rather than having too tight a management hierarchy;

- assigning the best talent to the most promising opportunities;

- maintaining the original culture as the workforce rapidly expands;

- expanding and upgrading the scope of the original business model.

Who follows

So who is going to follow any of these leaders? It's a question which Russell Houghton has experienced first hand, both in his time transforming performance at IMI and running programmes for high-growth ventures at MCE.

First, leaders have a clarity about what is they want to offer, he says, which they then translate into a set of stretching goals. 'They're good at putting a stake in the ground that seems a long way out. Then before you get there, they move it again to keep pushing the organization.'

They are brave enough to switch course if the vision isn't being met. It's not just about being tough, but empathetic too. They appreciate that it's going to upset people, but it has to be done, says Houghton. 'It's the understanding that it's hard, but it's with the vision in mind. If we don't achieve these goals, we aren't going to make the progress we want to make.'

It applies to people too. Growth relies on having the right people in the right place. 'You take a long, hard look at who they are and what they bring. You appreciate what your strengths are now and where the gaps are.'

At IMI, the chief executive was eventually succeeded by a graduate who had moved up through the business. 'You build a pipeline of talent so you have people who have the right understanding of the business and know how to make a profit.'

Securing the value

You can have the right solution for the right customer, but you won't fulfil your potential for growth, if you set your prices by taking your costs and adding ten percent. As Simon Sinek says, you are thinking 'inside out'. Your focus is on the what of your offer. Instead, look from the 'outside in' and see what is the true value you represent. It can come in many ways, not just price. It might be service. It might be reliability. It might be taking away risks. Your task is to find out these whys.

Instead of sales, says Russell Houghton, start to think of accounts, giving managers more power to co-ordinate design, production and marketing to create the best possible service. You will then be less prone to leaving money on the table. In sales, ground is often given too easily to win the business. Instead, you want to find the confidence to justify why you are charging a premium.

Account managers who can build business at this high level are those who 'listen loudly', says Russell Houghton. 'What are your customers not saying? Where are the gaps? What are the trends? You'll find out what they are really looking for and what more value you can offer. That's the difference you can make and how you can grow profitably.'

Illustration: leadership for growth
Statement by Elia Congiu, chief HR officer, MSC Cruises

'MSC Cruises has undergone a remarkable transformation over the past two decades. Since 2003, we've made a €16.6 billion investment in expanding our fleet. Originally focused on the Mediterranean, today our growth, innovation and adaptability has made us a global cruise industry leader. Our employee base has nearly doubled since

2017 to meet operational demands for crew and on shoreside. This diverse workforce is pivotal to our success and delivering exceptional onboard experiences.

'A significant milestone in our journey is the recent introduction of Explora Journeys, our luxury brand, which redefines onboard luxury with curated, immersive cruise experiences. This expansion reflects our agility in responding to trends and exceeding luxury travellers' expectations.

'Our growth story is not just about ships and destinations, but also about the talented individuals who make MSC Cruises what it is. With the introduction of new ships and the exploration of new markets, our employee count has seen a significant increase. This expansion brings along with it both excitement and challenges, especially when it comes to preserving our core identity amidst a more diverse and larger team. As we grow, the challenge lies in ensuring that every new team member becomes a custodian of this identity while also infusing their unique perspectives. It's about growth without compromise, innovation without losing sight of our roots.

'We've implemented a well-defined leadership competency model that outlines the specific skills and behaviours essential to supporting our growth endeavours. Effective communication is paramount. We consistently and transparently communicate our core values, emphasising their intrinsic alignment with our growth strategies. This approach ensures that our employees can readily discern the vital connection between our values and our overarching goals, thereby fostering a profound sense of purpose and direction. We also align individual and team goals to our objectives, reinforcing the central role of growth in our daily operations and decision-making.

'Preserving our values is a top priority. Our culture defines us, and leaders play a pivotal role in championing and preserving our values, making sure they remain a core part of our identity during rapid growth. Leadership development programmes are another cornerstone. These programmes equip our leaders with the skills not only to lead effectively but also to manage change and inspire their teams through growth-related transitions.'

Conclusion

So leadership for growth is about fully focusing the organization and the whole team to make sure people have it in mind in everything they do all the time. At any level or in any function, it creates a shared mindset. It is the background of the organization as a whole, driven by the leaders, communicated about regularly and acted on every day.

'I am fighting for growth' summarises a culture that leaders cascade through the organization. It is not only about communicating it. It is about much more. Whether it is your internal systems, your rewards, your feedbacks or your meeting agendas, they all align to growth.

Sources

- 'Start with why: how great leaders inspire', Simon Sinek, TedX Talks, YouTube, 2009
- 'Choosing to grow: The leader's blueprint', Michael Birshan, Biljana Cvetanovski, Rebecca Doherty, Tjark Freundt, Andre Gaeta, Greg Kelly, Erik Roth, Ishaan Seth, and Jill Zucker, McKinsey & Co, July 2022
- 'The ten rules of growth', Chris Bradley, Rebecca Doherty, Nicholas Northcote, and Tido Röder, McKinsey & Co, August 2022
- 'Are you a growth leader? The seven beliefs and behaviours that growth leaders share', Biljana Cvetanovski, Eric Hazan, Jesko Perrey, and Dennis Spillecke, McKinsey & Co, 2019
- *Exponential Organizations: Why new organizations are ten times better, faster and cheaper than yours*, Salim Ismail, Singularity University. 2014
- 'The Overlooked Key to a Successful Scale-up', Jeffrey F. Rayport, Davide Sola and Martin Krupp, Harvard Business Review, January-February 2023

Growth · Employee experience · Innovation · Diversity and inclusion · Partnerships · Business · People · Inspiration · LEADER'S DRIVERS · Digitalization · Customer focus · Process · Market · Effectiveness · Brands · Strategy execution · Personalization

3.

LEADERSHIP FOR INNOVATION

New solutions are being demanded of all organizations in how they respond to the digital revolution and the transformation of the workplace. Most of them accept that innovation is becoming an overarching imperative: over 80 percent of leaders surveyed by McKinsey & Co say it is one of their top three priorities. Yet most of them are disappointed in how it turns out: less then 10 percent say they are satisfied with how innovation is performing within their organizations.

So is it realistic for them to aspire to be innovators? or is it too far out of reach? are there better ways for them to go about it? and what difference can they make as leaders?

They are questions we discussed at MCE with a well-known maker of air conditioning. It found itself competing against a global titan, which had a seemingly infinite capacity for upgrades. How could they possibly reverse the slow but steady erosion of their market share?

What if they were to compare themselves more broadly, exploring the potential for innovation in other areas such as customer service, delivery or sales presence? Two options were identified for where they could be stronger. By redirecting their efforts in innovation, they have now started fighting their way back.

So innovation is best understood as a spectrum. At one end, radical new value can plainly be created with technology, as we are seeing in digital and life sciences. However, innovation is not just about new products or services, as many leaders mistakenly assume. Such a narrow view then involves them in heavy upfront costs in research and assembling a specialist team. However, that's just one top-down approach. There are many other options.

Innovation is widely accepted as creating or finding new value for your users. The inventor or the creator is the one who has the idea. The innovator, as the pioneering management guru Peter Drucker remarked, is the one who brings everything together and completes the circle of new value. In other words, the idea could have come from any number of different sources.

For makers of air conditioning and for everybody else, it is a much more expansive definition, which allows you to tap into the creative thinking in all areas of your business, not just one team of specialists. You align the whole company around innovation. At all levels, in all directions, you structure yourself to transform ideas into value, making that the foundation for how you reward people.

It is about creating a receptive culture that listens to the market, to your employees, to your suppliers and to your extended networks. You will find yourself in a flow of ideas about how to improve not just your products and services, but all your operations, systems and processes. The question now becomes how to turn them into worthwhile action.

Here we reach another limitation for leaders. In reality, many organizations are happier being operators in the present rather than innovators for the future. Let's call it the Netflix dilemma. In the market for films at home, you have beaten the then market leader, Blockbuster, into submission by delivering DVDs to watchers at home. Do you then drop this business and bet everything on streaming as a service?

In retrospect, we would all make the right call. In the moment, however, it's much harder and takes real courage. In most organizations, there will be someone who resists in favour of continuing with the current business.

For Frank de Keyzer, who leads on innovation in the MCE faculty, it is the 'yes but' syndrome. 'Yes but,' he says, 'is the same as no. Leaders are under such short-term pressure to deliver results, innovation is expected to work almost immediately, so there are always reasons to hesitate.'

'Innovation, however, always come with risk. If leaders can't tolerate failure, that's why innovation doesn't work too well. It's better to keep an open mind, start small, learn from your mistakes and accept there are many ways to innovate. As a leader, you are competing in the present, of course, but you are constantly creating your future business, whether you acknowledge it or not.'

Innovation radar

Many organizations allow themselves to adopt a mistakenly narrow view of innovation, often seeing it as the same as new product development or traditional research and development, says a paper in the *MITSloan Management Review* (Spring 2006). 'Such myopia can lead to the systematic erosion of competitive advantage, resulting in firms within an industry looking more similar to each other over time.'

Patterns develop in how they innovate: in tech, the focus is R&D; in chemicals, it is process; in consumer goods, it is brands. The trouble is that if they are all looking in the same place, they tend to come up with the same solutions.

In fact, innovation is far broader than product or tech innovation. As a leader who wants to drive it throughout the organization, it is about thinking of all the possible dimensions in which you can create value for customers in your business system. There are twelve in all under the headings of what, who, how and where:

- **What**: new offerings, common platforms, integrated solutions.

- **Who**: under-served customers, user experiences, value capture.

- **How**: operating processes, organizational scope, supply chain.

- **Where**: distribution channels, networks and brand leverage.

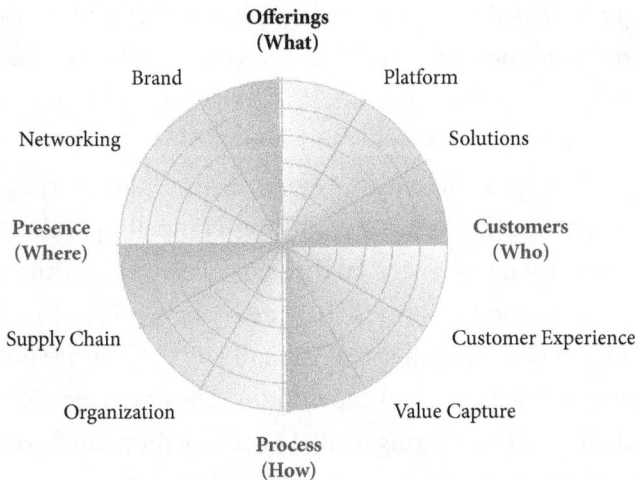

Figure 1: the innovation radar displays the twelve dimensions of business innovation, anchored by offerings, customers, processes and points of presence (MITSloan, 2006)

Each is a powerful source of innovation in its own right. By considering them all, leaders can take a much wider view of where the most valuable opportunities might lie, says the MITSloan paper: 'when a company identifies and pursues neglected innovation dimensions, it can change the basis of competition and leave other firms at a distinct disadvantage because each dimension requires a different set of capabilities that cannot be developed or acquired overnight'.

Red ocean, blue ocean

For a generation, the narrative about innovation has been dominated by disruption. As tech has turned markets and industries upside down, it has created a few spectacular winners, some heavy losers and billions of satisfied customers.

As a model, it's worth pursuing for those with the technical ingenuity and commercial agility. However, this contest over reconfiguring existing markets represents a red ocean, a highly competitive arena in which much blood will be spilt in determining the eventual winners.

For two professors at Insead, W. Chan Kim and Renée Mauborgne, the spectrum of innovation is much wider. In their book, *Blue Ocean Strategy* (Harvard Business Review Press, 2004), they argue for creating new market space by offering compelling value that makes their competition irrelevant. In this blue ocean, value innovators think in terms of the total solutions that customers seek, even it lies beyond the boundaries of what they traditionally offer. They are not looking to leverage existing assets and capabilities. They ask themselves what we would do if we were starting again? That way they can find unoccupied territory that represents a quantum leap in value.

Such innovation depends on opening up the whole organization and directing all your talent to exploring the market. Strategy becomes more collaborative, more visual and less numeric. For leaders, it takes courage to abandon the confines of traditional strategy and adopt such a wide-angle lens.

Now Kim and Mauborgne have turned their attention to 'non-disruptive creation' (*Harvard Business Review*, May-June 2023). As an example, they take Cunard, which was the largest passenger liner across the north Atlantic until the start of the jet age in the 1960s. It then reinvented itself for luxury vacations at sea, starting the modern cruise industry. Today it is part of the Carnival corporation which has revenues of $30 billion a year.

At the other end of the spectrum from disruption, it is possible, they say, to create new industries and jobs without anyone losing out. The emerging business for space tourism is such a case.

So, in adopting technologies such as artificial intelligence and blockchain, it is not necessarily just about winners and losers. Both ends of market-creating innovation matter equally: 'non-disruptive creation is an essential complement to disruption. Each has a role to play in building a compelling future'.

Better innovation

So how as a leader can you start to cascade such a culture of innovation through the organization? Recent research by McKinsey found that mastering innovation can generate profits 2.4 times higher than the norm (August 2022). In their survey of 183 companies' proficiency at innovation, they established the eight essential elements and the questions for leaders to ask:

- **Aspire**: is innovation-led growth critical to us and do we have a set of cascaded targets?

- **Choose**: do we run a coherent portfolio?

- **Discover**: can we turn R&D into value propositions?

- **Evolve**: are we creating profitable new business models?

- **Accelerate**: can we develop and launch an innovation quickly?

- **Scale**: can we launch at the right scale?

- **Extend**: can we leverage our networks?

- **Mobilise**: are our people ready to innovate repeatedly?

For leaders, the first two are critical: bold aspirations and tough choices. Otherwise efforts to innovate become too scattershot. For many leaders, McKinsey concludes, it means shifting their mindsets or management approaches.

'While many imagine that innovation is solely about creativity and generating ideas, at its core, innovation is a matter of resource allocation. To put it another way: it's one thing to frame innovation as a catalyst for growth, and another to act upon it by refocusing people, assets and management on the organization's best ideas.'

The possibility gap

So how can leaders adopt such an innovative mindset? For many, their priority is managing performance in the present. However, that is only one of three boxes that ultimately determine the fate of organizations, says one of the world's leading thinkers on strategy and innovation, Vijay Govindarajan, a professor at the Tuck Business School.

Far less weight is given to the other two. In box two, you selectively forget the past and change mindsets. In box three, you give yourself the creative scope to imagine the future and experiment with ideas. As a horizon, three years is too short for Govindarajan. You can probably give a reasonable estimate of what will change in your business and your market. Instead, set your sights ten years from now.

Technology will almost certainly have redefined and reshaped your business, making your customers, competitors and suppliers behave in new and unpredictable ways. Planning for this future is largely meaningless. Too much can happen. Preparing for it is what matters.

You are only likely to pick up weak signals. They might be background noise. They might be the next leap forward. You have to experiment, then be ready to abandon existing models and scale up fast.

Tension between the boxes is inevitable. Box one is all about efficiency and improving your current business model. You are responding to clear signals and linear changes. You can rely on incremental improvements and operational excellence, reducing any variance in performance and following the business plan closely.

In boxes two and three, you are thinking expansively and running irregular tests of your assumptions. 'You cannot close the possibility gap through quality or continuous improvement,' says Professor Govindarajan. 'The only way is through non-linear innovation, as so much is unknown and unknowable about the future.'

Creative culture

So, under the pressure of the present, it is easy to let the future slide. No one will notice at first. You will only feel the impact when someone else leaps ahead.

Nor can you expect to meet all the demands of the future on your own. You can't just leverage your current competencies. Instead, you will rely on opening up the organization, bringing in new skills.

It's similar to when I was giving speeches at universities a few years ago. I talked about the challenges of preparing students for technologies that have not been invented and for challenges that no one is thinking about yet. The environment in which they are going to operate is completely different from today's. During three or five years of study, everything can change. So, as a university, you have to cultivate the skills and the adaptability to identify and seize opportunities.

To focus a company on innovation, it is the same. Of course, you will require engineering and design. But critical thinking, openness and flexibility are equally essential. So leadership for innovation is about making sure that at every level people are ready to keep in mind ways to improve and are ready to look at the picture differently. You want to encourage and reward a culture that encourages the flow of ideas, that lets people shake things up and that dispels their fear of trying something new.

So can we learn anything about how to manage creativity from serial winners of awards for advertising and marketing campaigns? The Lions at the Cannes festival are among the most prestigious in the industry. In a study of the winners over 15 years, McKinsey observed that the top quartile were well ahead on three financial indicators (revenue growth, return to shareholders and enterprise value) and displayed four distinct management practices:

- Their leaders saw themselves as personally involved in delivering and encouraging creativity.

- They were near fanatical in understanding their customers, going way beyond standard research methods.

- They were ready to move quickly and deliver with clear goals.

- They recognised that a launch is just the start of gaining feedback and learning about a market.

Involving everyone

When half of the growth in most industries now relies on innovation, it can't just be left to specialists, says a recent report from AMA

Global, *Innovation: a critical necessity*. 'The era of hyper-innovation has arrived and it's time for everyone to get involved.'

Even in a sector seen as traditionally low tech and competitive as fast foods, innovation is at the core of how an operator like McDonald's is transforming its customer experience (through mobile ordering and voice recognition, for instance), as well as rewriting its menus for the 2020s.

Despite such examples, many organizations continue to overlook the largest and most natural sources of ideas: their workforces. AMA reports that four in ten employees have had an idea which they didn't bother to put forward.

Leaders below the level of chief executive are equally indifferent: only 27 percent in Europe, the Middle East and Africa consider innovation part of their job. In return, only 22 percent of employees think their leaders would actively encourage ideas from them. So what can be done, asks AMA?

- Like McDonald's make sure innovation is consistently viewed as part of everyone's job. It runs a global hackathon open to anyone in the company ready to share their disruptive thinking and entrepreneurial spirit.

- Share knowledge freely with employees: data, feedback and collaborations all spark creative thinking.

- Recognise when ideas are put forward, regardless of what happens to them.

- Create the psychological safety for people to feel comfortable in sharing ideas.

- Actively support the advancement of viable ideas: it sends a powerful signal that it is worth putting them forward.

- Treat viable ideas with urgency: it is demotivating when action is slow to happen.

Today's leaders, the AMA report concludes, 'cannot possibly foresee and prepare for every potential challenge ahead, but they can enhance their organization's readiness to react with novel, creative solutions and a willingness and determination to realise them.'

Illustration: creating innovation solutions at Knauf Insulation
Statement by Abdelmoula el Hadi, head of innovation excellence, EMEA/ APAC, Knauf Insulation, one of the world's largest manufacturers of insulation products and solutions

'We are a forward-thinking organization with a mission to challenge conventional thinking and create innovative solutions that not only improve our living and building environments but also prioritise the wellbeing of all who make and use them. We actively challenge industry norms, striving to pioneer new concepts and perspectives on insulation and building practices. Our commitment lies in crafting innovative solutions that redefine industry standards, emphasising quality, performance and sustainability. Ultimately, our focus extends beyond business; it centres on our people, customers, communities and the planet we all share.

'Innovation is of paramount importance in our business because it is the driving force that keeps us ahead of the competition. It encompasses much more than R&D; it's our response to the relentless demand for improvement. In a highly competitive industry, we must demonstrate leadership not only in our technology but also in our systems and solutions. Innovation is the compass guiding us toward sustainable growth and the transformation of our industry.

'We foster an innovation focus throughout our organization by placing a strong emphasis on knowledge development, ideation and front-end innovation. We actively encourage our employees to engage in creative problem-solving and innovative thinking. We believe that everyone within the entire organization plays a role in shaping our innovative future. We allocate dedicated time and resources for R&D projects, actively involve employees in idea generation, and promote continuous learning and skills development.

'Our leaders play a crucial role in cascading innovation throughout the organization. Key success factors in their management of innovation drivers include setting clear innovation objectives; prioritising and allocating resources effectively; and actively promoting a culture of curiosity, experimentation, rapid prototyping and risk-taking. They lead by example and empower teams to bring forward innovative ideas and initiatives.

'We do acknowledge hurdles and difficulties when it comes to change. As we embrace innovation, there can be some slight resistance from established practices and resource allocation can be a challenge. However, we view these hurdles as opportunities for growth and improvement, and we invest in effective change management strategies to overcome them.

'The links between an innovation culture and the performance of our company are undeniable. We continuously monitor and assess the impact of our innovation initiatives on company performance. For instance, our innovation ratio over the last five years demonstrates the significant contributions of innovative solutions to our turnover percentages. We also believe that innovation and sustainability must go hand in hand. By aligning these two, we not only drive company performance but also contribute positively to a more sustainable future.'

Sources

- 'The 12 Different Ways for Companies to Innovate', Monanbir Sawhey, Robert C
- Wolcott and Inigo Arroniz, *MIT Sloan Management Review*, Spring 2006
- *Blue Ocean Strategy: How to create uncontested market space and make the competition irrelevant*, W. Chan Kim and Renée Mauborgne, Harvard Business Review Press, 2004
- *Beyond Disruption: Innovate and achieve growth without displacing industries, companies or jobs*, W. Chan Kim and Renée Mauborgne, Harvard Business Review Press, 2023
- 'Innovation doesn't have to be disruptive: create new markets for growth without destroying existing companies or jobs', W. Chan Kim and Renée Mauborgne, *Harvard Business Review*, May/June 2023
- 'What is innovation?', McKinsey Explainers, McKinsey & Co, August 2022
- *The three-box solution: a strategy for leading innovation*, Professor Vijay Govindarajan, Harvard Business Review Press, April 2016
- 'Creativity's bottom line: how winning companies turn creativity into business value and growth', Marc Brodherson, Jason Heller, Jesko Perrey, and David Remley, McKinsey Digital, June 2017

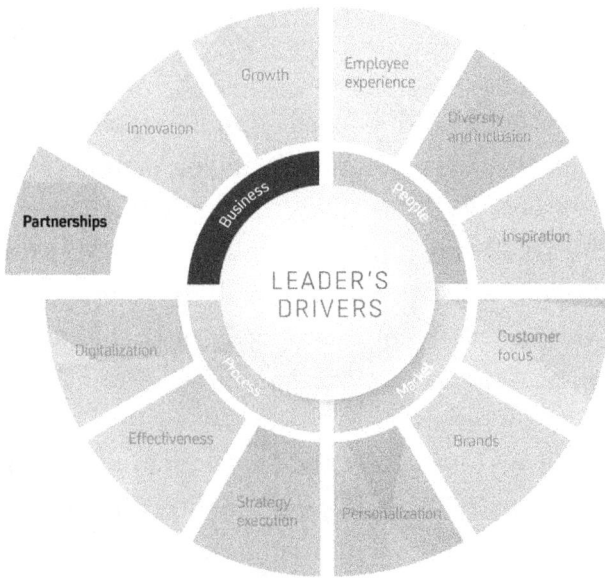

Growth

Employee experience

Innovation

Diversity and inclusion

Partnerships

Business

People

Inspiration

LEADER'S DRIVERS

Digitalization

Customer focus

Effectiveness

Market

Brands

Strategy execution

Personalization

4.

LEADERSHIP FOR PARTNERSHIPS

Partnerships are becoming more than a support act, as they start to occupy a central role in creating new value and opening up growth. Consumer electronics took an early lead. Pharmaceuticals is now following.

In both cases, they have realised that no one can expect to follow a heroic model for making discoveries and building operations on their own anymore. Networks of value have become too widely distributed and too transparent. Advantage lies in accelerating access to new ideas, breakthrough technologies, scarce resources and smart people, whether they are inside or outside your organization.

You might once have relied on acquiring a capability and bringing it under your control. However, as a model, it is proving too static, too costly and too risky. Instead, partnerships are becoming a strategic priority for research, production, supply and promotion.

How they perform depends on how they are led. There are multiple ways in which partnerships can go wrong and it is fair to assume that 50 percent of them will fail. The challenge for leaders is how they align teams who have different assumptions, different incentives and different cultures. A sense of unity is hard to achieve and even harder to sustain. That's just between two individual partners.

In reality, partnerships within the digital economy are becoming more open and intense. Take a typical supply chain. Once it linked together as a sequence of separate relationships. In Industry 4.0, the whole supply chain is digitally visible in real time to everyone, creating many more different points of interaction. Direction becomes harder to maintain and value is easily lost.

In such circumstances, a new form of leadership is required, says Frédéric Ollier, a senior MCE associate who used to run partnerships for Sanofi, the leading French pharmaceutical company. 'You share the leadership with those outside your organization. As a co-leader, you align your objectives and create transparency, putting in checks and balances to keep your strategy on track.'

The challenge is not just to keep on top of each partnership, but to master them all as a strategic discipline, so you have a view of how they are all performing. You can then spot where extra value can be created within this network of relationships.

An early example was Philips' partnership with Sara Lee to catch the demand for the luxury brewing of coffee at home. Within four years, its Senseo system for making your own cappuccino or expresso had ten million users. Philips then turned what it had leant into PerfectDraft, a partnership for pouring beer at home with AB InBev.

This capacity to lead partnerships is becoming a competitive advantage in its own right. In pharmaceuticals, it is being used to accelerate innovation. In consumer goods, it is opening up a new channel to growth, as the novelty of digital advertising plateaus.

Innovation partnerships

In medicine, a combination of digital and genomics is transforming innovation. The classical models of discovery and commercialization are being superseded, as artificial intelligence speeds up diagnoses, biotechs target more personalized treatments and data creates profiles more individual to each patient.

The industry is learning to operate in niches and becoming closer to users. A more open, collaborative culture is being adopted in which partners combine to create treatments at speed, as in the case of Covid, or medicines more personal to each of our genetic profiles.

Value is dispersed more widely through the chain of research, production, supply and use. Each partner, particularly if they are backed by venture capital, will expect to share on the upside of bringing a treatment into widespread medical use.

So the nature of these partnerships is intensifying, says Frédéric Ollier, who was responsible for a collaboration with a Dutch biotech when he was at Sanofi. 'Before you might rely on licensing ideas and technologies with a view to an eventual acquisition. Now the interdependencies are more complex. It is up to leaders to create a sense of unity from different cultures and competing priorities.'

Growth partnerships

In consumer goods, bloggers and influencers are just one aspect of how growth is now generated. They are part of a wider emergence of 'a consumercentric ecosystem' that operates through partnerships, argues David Yovano in *The Partnership Economy*, a book about finding new customers, growing revenue and creating exceptional experiences (Wiley, 2022).

Such partnerships sprang up following the implosion of digital advertising, which had disregarded the customer experience and channelled everything through Big Tech. The disruptive response is a search for deeper, more authentic connections, which consumers feel they can trust.

As well as bloggers and influencers, referral partnerships reflect today's customer preferences and journeys, says Yovano. 'Business are operating in an environment of consumer scepticism and lack of trust in their media, advertising and sales.'

Partnerships are becoming a game-changer that allows companies to expand their capabilities far beyond what they can achieve on their own, he says: as partners, they share the same or similar target customers, coming together to create value for them in a collaborative, transparent and mutually rewarding way.

These referrals and recommendations can take many forms. It might just be an email. Or it could be an app or website integration.

Such partnerships are now more than a sideshow. For those who master them, they are becoming a channel that constitutes 28 percent of their revenue, reports Yovano.

Their efforts, he says, are 'supported by a strong, broad organizational commitment to partnerships as a growth strategy … and the right alignment among the necessary people, processes and technology to bring the strategy to life'.

Partnership skills

So as assumptions about innovation are rewritten and referrals take up the slack left by digital advertising, what are the skills expected of you as one of Frédéric Ollier's new leaders of partnerships?

Strategic mindset

As you scan your competitive environment, you are alive to the interdependencies in your ecosystem and see the value in forming a cross-functional, multi-disciplinary response. 'Without this collaborative mindset, you are limiting your chances to grow,' says Ollier.

In his own experience of industrial partnerships, outcomes rest on how clear your objectives are in your own mind, how far you can establish a genuinely common strategy and whether you can align a partnership around a set of key performance indicators. If such partnerships are to become a driver for you, then it will rely on establishing a process for finding and aligning them.

The right partner

Partners were once found by chief executives after sitting next to someone on the plane. Instead, it's better to draw on a range of perspectives and line up several possibilities who could improve your competitive performance.

Of course, you will check whether candidates have the right products and the right capabilities. However, it is worth going much deeper, says Ollier. In particular, is it possible for your cultures to combine? For instance, biotech ventures will operate more quickly, but may make short cuts that pharma would never contemplate.

You have to account for different behaviours and values at each stage of the partnership in a way you never would in your own organization: it is up to you to track and overcome these difficulties.

So you will define the right type of partner for you by what they can bring. Once you have these criteria, you can draw up a list of candidates, rather than making a reactive jump at opportunities.

Transparency, communication and trust

As a leader, your responsibility is not just to your own organization but to everyone within the partnership. You would like all involved to have a clear grasp of your strategy and communicate openly with each other. In practice, such transparency remains consistently difficult to achieve. You will find that trust is less than automatic. Some suspicion is inevitable across organizations. Nor is your legitimacy to speak always recognised. So communication becomes essential in confronting misunderstandings and doubts.

Cascading governance

Governance is not just about supervision at the top level. Nor is it about setting up a series of committees. You can't have a structure that overwhelms, particularly in partnerships between larger and smaller organizations. Instead, it's about creating day-to-day relationships between all the functions that are going to make the partnership work: research, production, marketing and finance. That way you can anticipate the inevitable challenges that you are going to encounter. Within your organization, you would also like to have someone whose focus is 100 percent on how partnerships as a whole are performing.

Value adjustments

At each level of the partnership, you would hope there is the potential for more value to be created than you originally expected. Ideally, you will negotiate adjustments to your strategy and your rewards in real time. If everyone shares the same mindset, it can happen. In practice, many partnerships either founder at this point or one ends up being bought out. The differences between them become too complex to resolve.

The end in mind

Within your own organization, it is rare that you will actively think about how it all might end. In partnerships, it is always worth keeping in mind. How is your partner going to evolve? what happens if the partnership loses its appeal? or if the competitive environment changes?

As a leader, you are always ready to analyse and reassess. This ability to transform the partnership is what gives you the best chance of securing its value and minimising its risk of failing.

In Ollier's case, the partnership he was leading between Sanofi and a smaller Dutch biotech came to an end after a separate and much larger acquisition raised questions about anti-trust in the United States. For both partners, the simplest solution was for Sanofi to acquire the rights from its Dutch colleagues.

Three degrees of partnership

The attention of leaders is usually first drawn to the potential of maximising individual partnerships. However, it only represents the first degree of value, say Henrich Greve, Tim Rowley and Andrew Shipilov in *Network Advantage* (Jossey-Bass, 2014). More value can be created, they argue, by taking a wider view of all the relationships within your portfolio and within your industry.

At the second degree of value, you will review all your existing partners, as well as the connections they have with each other. Taken together, they determine the extent to which power, co-operation and information flow across your network.

Essentially, you find two distinct types of portfolio: either hub and spoke where you operate at the centre and which favours you if you are making radical innovations; or integrated when all the partners are connected together, which will suit you when managing complex projects or making incremental improvements.

In the third degree, you expand your view to all the connections within your industry. Once you can see all those who are best connected, you can build your own status as a partner and enhance your reputation as a collaborator. A positive evaluation by others will improve your access to information, co-operation and power within your network.

You can also map out the potential to bring existing partners together to create new sources of value with you. Or, without revealing anyone's identity, make the case for how you could all collaborate with a high-status partner you don't have any ties with as yet.

Some organizations might choose to set up a partnership office to share this knowledge. Others expect their managers to reach out and report back, supported by knowledge management systems. In both cases, as a leader, you are less likely to find yourself struggling to find the right partner or feel that you are stuck in the wrong kind of portfolio of partnerships, if you have a wider strategic view of the networks in which you operate.

Illustration: partnerships at Debiopharm

Partnerships are the foundation for how Debiopharm has operated since it started in 1979. It occupies the space between the discovery and commercialization of new medical treatments. In its current portfolio, it has two established blockbusters and hopes to introduce another one in 2024. Eleven other products are in the pipeline, mostly in its traditional areas of strength of oncology and anti-infectives.

During the past 40 years, Debiopharm developed solid expertise in small molecules, ADC technologies and sustained-release formulations. Its strategy is to license and acquire early-stage assets from the research base, then take them through the phases of clinical testing and development, before finding a commercial partner to launch as a product.

In forming partnerships with researchers, it's a balance between negotiating terms and keeping them involved, says Nicolas Favre, director of business development at Debiopharm. 'We want to keep them in the loop and share in the rewards if it does work.'

Similarly, close relations are now being built with its commercial partners. 'We have shifted mindset. We are not just the challenger reminding them we have a contract. We are actively looking to help them as well, leveraging our particular areas of expertise. Once you are seen as a partner, it bears fruit later.'

Recently, Favre was involved in resetting a relationship that had lasted since 1986. 'It's like a marriage that has its ups and downs. We put everything on the table and started from a blank page. It's not about the past anymore, but what is happening today. You have to keep an open mind.'

For Favre, partnerships ultimately depend on trust. 'That's easy to say when you have a similar mindset. Innovation comes from many sources now. So you take the time not just to look at the asset, but the people involved.'

The more transparent you can be with each other, the easier it is later. 'Whatever high hopes that anyone might have, the reality is that most partnerships will fail. You don't want things to become tricky.'

'Or if you do reach a turning point and renegotiate what happens next, it's best to be clear about your objectives. For us, as a family business, it's about building for the long term, rather than selling up now.'

Conclusion

As Debiopharm is learning, the best results from partnerships come when you act as a co-leader. You have to be open enough and transparent enough to keep the relationship moving forward, adjusting to new priorities and expectations, whether it is time to wind down, scale up or spin out. As a leader, you are likely to find yourself with less control than usual and your partners may have different assumptions from yours, so you are going to find yourself relying on your powers to negotiate, persuade and collaborate to unlock the accelerated value that partnerships can bring. Equally, if partnerships are to become one of your drivers, you will make your teams comfortable operating with all the externals. As a leader, your role is to move forward in the same direction with people who have different horizons.

Sources

- *The Partnership Economy: How modern businesses find new customers, grow revenues and deliver exceptional experiences*, David Yovano, Wiley, 2022
- *Network Advantage: How to unlock value from your alliances and partnerships*, Henrich Greve, Tim Rowley and Andrew Shipilov, Jossey-Bass, 2014

PART 2

PROCESS

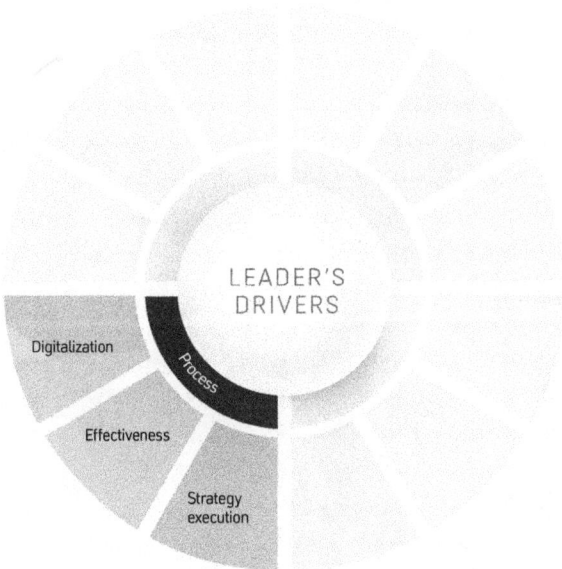

LEADER'S
DRIVERS

Process

Digitalization

Effectiveness

Strategy
execution

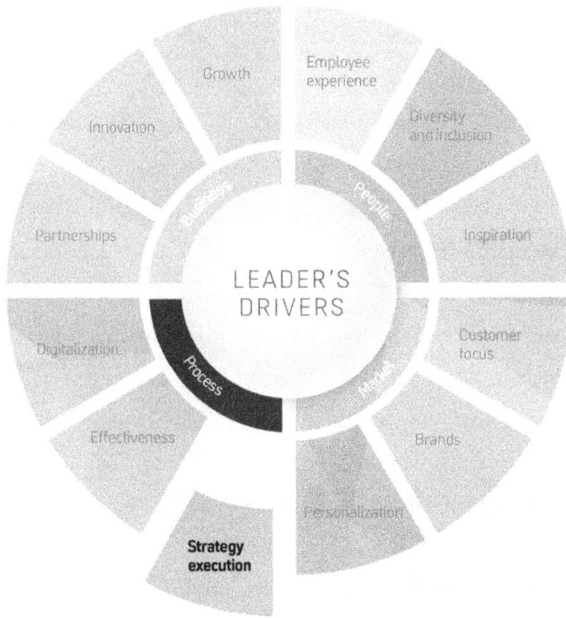

Growth · Employee experience · Innovation · Diversity and inclusion · Partnerships · Inspiration · LEADER'S DRIVERS · Digitalization · Customer focus · Effectiveness · Brands · Strategy execution · Personalization · Process · People · Market

5.

LEADERSHIP FOR STRATEGY EXECUTION

Are we quick enough in delivering value to our users? It's a question that haunts many leaders. For all their good intentions in upping their game and making improvements, results regularly fall well below where they would like them to be. It is estimated that 70 percent of strategies fail. In the case of mergers and acquisitions, it is even worse: 80 percent don't live up to expectations and 50 percent actually end up destroying value.

The strategy itself may be flawed, of course. That's true 20 percent of the time, says Ramesh Fatania on the MCE faculty and a former director at BP, who oversaw the integration of a major acquisition and then its disposal five years later. The remaining 80 percent of failures are down to faulty implementation. 'It's not a question of reaching for

51

perfection,' he says. 'It's a question of aligning yourself so decisions can be taken at speed.'

For John Browne, BP's chief executive in the 2000s, it was about giving future leaders the confidence to act. Fatania recalls a colleague who after spotting a rise in the costs of tankers, went straight ahead and expanded BP's fleet, saving the company billions when the prices then spiked. When you can align your strategic intent with operational implementation, then a series of benefits follow, whether by being able to anticipate changes in market direction or building a can-do culture.

It's the difference we often see between newcomers and incumbents. The newcomer dedicates itself to make itself lean and fast enough to change market expectations and give itself a chance of becoming a new type of number one. The incumbent is slow to notice what is happening, then takes its time to form a top-down response. When it then tries to play by the new rules, no one has the confidence to take decisions without approval. Their strategic thinking might be the best that money can buy, but as an organization it has become too slow to react.

Misaligned value

At MCE, it's a pattern we see all the time. I was once working with a global trader in commodities which called up MCE for a major transformation project. It wanted to change its strategy from competing on price to supporting buyers to make the best buy. More precisely, they wanted to help their clients optimise the use of the commodities they were buying. Clear enough. But what it did mean for its traders who were used to working in intensely competitive markets? how were they expected to behave now? and how were they were going to be rewarded?

A major global bank was looking to make the same sort of switch. Its 2000 investment advisors were going to stop pushing financial products and start designing the best packages for customers: as relationship managers, they would know their customers better. Great in theory again, although numerous misunderstandings could happen in practice.

It's not enough to cascade well thought-out strategies down the organization. Communication soon becomes disconnected from reality when managers, traders or advisors don't understand what it really means for them and what actions they are expected to take.

Often the solution is to send them on a course. But is that the solution? No one is going to solve a problem with competitive pricing by taking a negotiation course, for example. It is only the tip of the iceberg. First, let's see what can be done to compete.

Instead, it is about understanding the consequences of redefining your value proposition. Whether it's for innovation, price or customer intimacy, the implications for what to learn and how to behave are completely different. Whichever the strategy, negotiation is unlikely to be any more critical than any other business skill.

The discipline of market leaders

The risk for companies is that they condemn themselves to mediocre performance, while continuously striving to catch up competitively. In *The Discipline of Market Leaders*, Michael Treacy and Fred Wiersema argue that it is better to learn to play by a new set of competitive rules followed by market leaders. First published in the 1990s, their conclusions still ring true today.

'By relentlessly driving themselves to deliver extraordinary levels of distinctive value to carefully selected groups, market leaders make it impossible for other companies to compete on the old terms.'

First, they establish a unique proposition, combining values such as price, quality, performance or convenience. Then they create an operating model, combining processes, systems, structures and culture, that gives a company the capacity to deliver on its value proposition.

'If a company is going to achieve and sustain dominance, it must first decide where it will stake its claim in the market and what kind of value it will offer its customers. Then it can identify core competencies and re-engineer the processes that make up the operating model required to get the job done.'

Now, as then, there are numerous companies struggling to adapt to this competitive reality, whose 'stumbling performances provide cautionary tales about survival'.

Eight errors

So how is it still proving so hard for leaders to make good their strategic intentions and make fundamental changes to their organizations? In an article in the *Harvard Business Review* in the Spring of 1995, 'Leading change: why transformation efforts fail', Professor John Kotter saw change, whether as an acquisition or a turnaround, as a series of phases in which leaders can make one of eight errors. Any missteps, he argued, ultimately lead to a loss of momentum, even if the illusion of speed in temporarily maintained.

Change begins with a sense of urgency. Paralysis at the top comes from having too many managers and not enough leaders. So phase one 'goes nowhere until enough real leaders are promoted or hired into senior-level jobs'.

Teamwork at the top is the foundation for a guiding coalition that will have the strength to withstand resistance. Together, the leaders will develop a vision of the future that is easy to communicate, otherwise they will find change dissolving into incompatible projects. In their words and their actions, they will then communicate it day to day through every possible channel.

You want to embolden people to try new approaches and develop new ideas, so any obstacles in their way have to go. It might be a question of structure. It might be someone resisting change. Action is essential otherwise doubts start to grow.

Some short-term wins will maintain momentum. However, declaring victory too early can be catastrophic. Instead, each gain leads to the next challenge. Renewal takes years.

Ultimately, the change will only fully happen when it becomes part of the culture. It will be clear to everyone how new behaviours impact performance and the next generation of leaders will personify the new approach.

'In reality, even successful change efforts are messy and full of surprises,' says Kotter. 'Fewer errors can spell the difference between success and failure.'

Strategy to performance

Financially, such errors are damaging: on average, strategies deliver 63 percent of their promised value, according to research by Michael C Mankins and Richard Steele at Maradon for a 2005 article in the *Harvard Business Review*, 'Turning Great Strategy into Performance'.

'Even worse,' they say, 'the causes of this strategy-to-performance gap are all but invisible to top management. Leaders then pull the wrong levers in their attempts to turn around performance, pressing for better execution when they actually need a better strategy or opting to change direction when they should really focus the organization on execution. The result: wasted energy, lost time and continued underperformance'.

So how do market leaders perform in discerning causes and taking corrective action? 'Rather than improving their planning and execution processes separately, raising standards for both planning and execution simultaneously and creating clear links between them.'

For Maradon and Steele, it depends on following seven rules:

- making strategy concrete, not abstract;

- debating assumptions, not forecasts;

- creating a common language for different business units and disciplines;

- making an early and realistic start on lining up resources;

- giving executives a clear sense of their priorities;

- using real-time indicators to track performance;

- developing and rewarding the right people.

'The prize for closing the strategy-to-performance gap is huge: an increase in performance from 60 percent to 100 percent for most companies. But this almost certainly understates the true benefits. Companies that create tight links between their strategies, their plans and, ultimately, their performance, often experience a cultural multiplier effect.'

At MCE, such potential is realised in two ways: alignment through the creation of a 'strategy house' and implementation through a framework for execution.

The strategy house

We were once talking to a global head of logistics for a major consumer brand, who was struggling to implement a strategy. We ran a workshop for his team and realised that a perfectly good high-level strategy was not being translated into actions at the level of divisions and units. Managers didn't realise how it related to them. So nothing was getting done.

'It's one of the biggest areas where strategies get blocked,' says Ramesh Fatania. 'It's not intentional. No one is suppressing it. It's just not registering as a priority for action.'

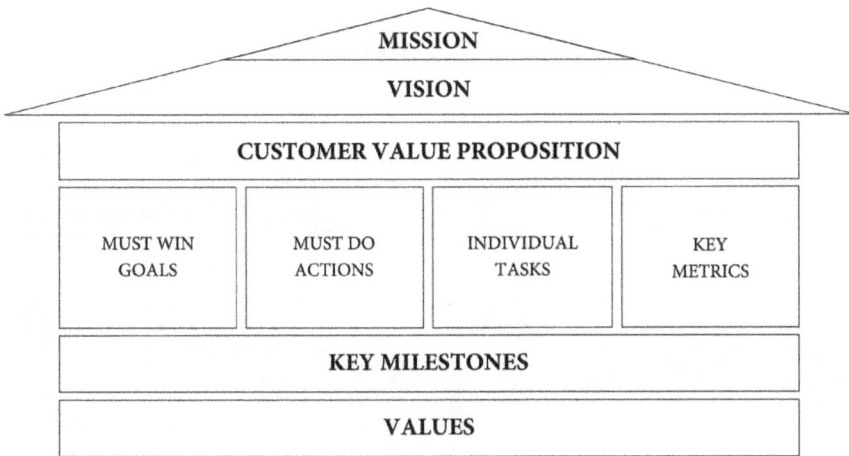

| MISSION |
| VISION |

| CUSTOMER VALUE PROPOSITION |
| MUST WIN GOALS | MUST DO ACTIONS | INDIVIDUAL TASKS | KEY METRICS |
| KEY MILESTONES |
| VALUES |

Figure 1: the strategy house (source: MCE)

'So how do you resolve it? At the top you have your mission and vision, at the bottom you have your value, in the middle you have your strategies, actions and metrics, which are summarised into milestones. You then break all these down into terms that correspond to each division or unit, a series of baby strategy houses.'

'It's a diligent, painstaking process of alignment,' says Fatania. 'You're planning, you're conferring, you're adjusting. It puts you in a stronger position at the start, then you can use it to track performance as you go.'

Execution framework

Around this series of strategy houses, you then build a framework for implementation around six interlocking elements: customer value, leadership, organization, metrics, strategy commitment and culture. In combination, they reinforce each other creating a powerful cumulative effect.

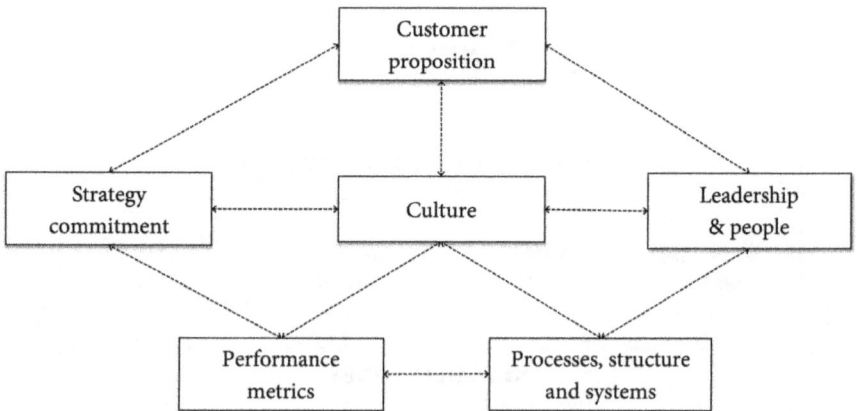

Figure 2: the execution framework (source: MCE)

Customer value

The type of strategic action you take is determined by the value proposition you adopt for your customers. Any lack of clarity inevitably leads to strategic drift. Essentially, you will operate in one of four segments:

- price through efficient operations;

- premium offer through quality;

- in-between through loyalty or regulation;

- custom made through expertise to create off-the-shelf solutions.

Each has different consequences for your processes and your metrics, which can cause confusion if you are trying to change from one to another.

Leadership

At every level of your organization, you want leaders to be involved and visible, explaining again and again why a change is being made. Why are we doing this? And why is it going be better for all of us?

You will give these leaders a clear mandate for change and hold them accountable, even writing a performance clause into their contracts. You will delegate as much authority to them as possible, so speedy decisions can be taken and they are able to allocate resources effectively. Finally, they will have the confidence to operate horizontally, not just vertically, bringing different functions together.

Commitment

Six Cs will build commitment to the change you are making: context, clarity, candour, constructive, consistency, continuous. 'Don't dress it up,' says Ramesh Fatania. 'People will see straight through you. Make it straightforward and simple. Be honest about what's broken and needs fixing.'

'Set up your communications strategy from day one. Then keep doing it. Otherwise people will start to think it no longer matters.'

Metrics

If you are switching your value proposition, then the metrics of how you are performing can be hard to follow. For instance, if you had been a transactional supplier, then you would have made sales your primary target. If you are now looking to build premium relationships, how do you now measure and reward the sales team, so the right behaviours are now encouraged?

Take care to make sure you get the whole picture by following both leading and lagging indicators. Leading indicators are activity based and easy to follow. Lagging indicators are based on outcomes and the assumptions you are making. They are messier. So, for instance, you might know how many people are due to leave a company. However, the benefits will depend how and when their departure happens.

More companies are now adopting balanced scorecards. Instead of just relying on financial indicators, three others are adopted: customer satisfaction, employee satisfaction and process improvements. All four are linked to rewards and incentives.

Processes, structures and systems

Your processes, structures and systems are the glue that creates the agility, the speed and the collaboration on which the implementation of your strategy depends. It is easy for them to become fossilised. You don't want to over-engineer them or under-engineer them, says Ramesh Fatania. 'Instead, you want to link up your strategy, so make sure you are continuously scrubbing them out and keeping the focus on how you are actually delivering value to your users.'

Culture

You are going to have to live your strategy and inspire your people to follow it. That's why the observation that 'culture eats strategy for breakfast', attributed to the pioneer of management thinking, Peter Drucker, is still so widely in circulation.

A change in your culture can happen in two ways, says Ramesh Fatania. 'As a leader, you can make the case for the new ways of thinking and new ways of behaving that a strategy requires. That's inside out.'

'Culture also changes from the outside in. Your whole framework for implementation will inevitably impact culture and change everyone's day-to-day habits. Everything is interconnected. It's an ecosystem for change that you have created, where the results depend on leadership and enabling people.'

For me, one of the best examples of aligning teams to deliver a consistently high level of performance is Colruyt Group, whose skills in implementing strategies have allowed it to keep competing on price for 50 years.

Illustration: keeping the promise of lowest prices
Statement by the Colruyt Group

'The Colruyt Group is a family business that has grown over three generations into a retail group with over 33,000 employees and a diverse portfolio of food and non-food formats in Belgium, France and Luxembourg which made revenues of €10.8 billion in 2022/23. The biggest activity remains our supermarket Colruyt, which has delivered on its brand promise of lowest prices day after day for 50 years. Since then, we have diversified our activities substantially.

However, we remain true to retail, which still accounts for four-fifths of our revenue.

'As the only 100 percent Belgian retailer, Colruyt Group continues to invest in logistics and production in our own country. We buy as much as possible from Belgian producers, contributing to the sustainability of agriculture and the anchoring of craftsmanship. We champion a fair and competitive landscape in which integrated and independent stores continue to coexist perfectly, without unfair competition in wages and working conditions.

'Today, we are active in ten retail formats with both physical outlets and online shops. In addition, we operate in food service and wholesale. In recent years, we have also grown strongly as a producer and supplier of renewable wind and solar energy. Finally, it is typical of Colruyt Group that we continue to do many things ourselves. We possess a wealth of experience and expertise in areas such as technology, IT and communication, as well as production and packaging of meat, coffee, cheese and wine.

'At Colruyt Group, we want to make a positive difference with everything we do. At every stage of life and at all important moments in our customers' lives, we want to be there for them in a suitable way. For this reason, we aim for maximum complementarity between our different brands. One by one, they differentiate themselves with simple solutions for specific requirements. Each in their own, authentic way, our brands express the "simplicity in retail" that we represent as Colruyt Group.

'The lowest price for each product at every moment: for 50 years now, it has been our promise to which the brand Colruyt Lowest Prices remains true even in difficult circumstances. In the past financial year, rising raw materials, energy, packaging and transport prices made the annual supplier negotiations even more challenging. Colruyt took the necessary time to work out solutions acceptable to all parties in constructive discussions, always with an eye for both the lowest price guarantee and the long-term relationships with its suppliers.

'After years of double-digit growth, we are now experiencing a period of slowdown. This is not uncommon, especially in a context of high inflation that is seriously challenging all retailers and has sharply increased our costs. Colruyt fulfils its promise of lowest prices by working efficiently and focusing on lowest costs, for example with sober shop fittings, energy-efficient freezers and fully loaded trucks.

'Our company's success is determined by the skills, attitudes and knowledge of our employees and their teams. At Colruyt Group we have a common purpose; we want to create sustainable added value together through value-driven craftsmanship in retail. Only together with our colleagues, suppliers, business partners, investors and customers can we make a positive difference.

'We always start with a positive view of people. We believe in people's creative power to see and seize opportunities. We assume that every employee is driven to deliver quality and can add something to the greater whole. So, we do all we can to allow our employees' natural life energy to flow as effectively as possible. That stimulates their entrepreneurship and growth in their craft and as people. After all, as the people grow, our company will grow.

'For us, sustainable entrepreneurship means doing business without mortgaging the future. Through a wide variety of small and large initiatives, the company wants to make a positive difference so as to ensure that future generations can experience and enjoy the beauty the planet has to offer.

'In stormy times, it is the roots that determine how firmly our tree stands. Results are merely a consequence. They merely tell us something about how we performed in a given context. That's why, at Colruyt Group, we don't focus on results but on goals. That means setting a goal and doing the right thing towards it in the here and now. We are focused, have confidence in our own ability and hope for the best possible outcome. Not by concentrating on the fruits, but by staying focused on our orchard and looking after our *terroir*.

'As a retail company, customer trust is key to us. We therefore want to continue to meet their wishes and needs and make life easier for them, now and in the future. The main customer needs we want to focus on are budget, sustainability, health and convenience. Customers want to be able to choose the offer that suits them best at any time.

'In the years to come, Colruyt Group has the ambition to continue to grow, gain further expert knowledge and provide a sustainable offering in each of its four areas of expertise (food, health and wellbeing, non-food and energy). To give more concrete form to our ambitions and objectives, we have formulated four strategic changes, on which we will be focusing strongly in the coming years:

- Being the most cost-efficient retailer in our stores, logistics and support services, by focusing on economies of scale, automation and digitalization. In this way, we can offer a high-quality, correctly priced basic range on a permanent basis.

- Being a 'phygital' retailer, in which the physical and the digital reinforce each other, using data to lead the way in online shopping.

- Being the best retailer for our customers, through skills excellence in all our activities.

- Growing further by responding to opportunities for new synergies and commercial formats, including in city concepts, in France and Luxembourg, in B2B, in digital business etc.

'At Colruyt Group, we greatly value the insights and experience that three generations of entrepreneurship have brought us. We know who we are, what we stand for together, we appreciate our own strengths, identity and culture. In this way, we manage to keep a family atmosphere and an SME attitude as a company that now has more than 33,000 employees.

'In such a large organization, it is a challenge for everyone to know and feel what their contribution makes in the bigger picture. Hence, in addition to investing in tech, just as much attention is paid to culture and identity: who are we together?'

Conclusion

Change is an emotional experience, which typically goes through four stages. As a leader, you want to minimise the highs and lows, bringing everyone with you. The first reaction to change is rational: often felt as excitement, sometimes as denial. At this point, people will want information from you.

As the reality of the change sets in, feelings change to confusion, anger or frustration. It's easy to lose some of your best people during this phase, particularly during mergers, so your support as a leader is what matters most.

Those who remain now move into acceptance and will be ready to explore new ways of thinking, although they will be looking for direction from you. Finally, they will commit to the change and will be relying on you for encouragement.

Essentially, you will find yourself dealing with people in four camps: 15 percent are navigators who will embrace the change and 15 percent are conservatives who will resist it. In the middle, you have 70 percent who are bystanders or critics, whose attitude will ultimately be determined by how you communicate with them.

That's why your ability as a leader to explain the context matters so much: why are we doing this? what are the consequences? what is the intent? what are we going to do? As a leader, what matters is this ability to align your systems and processes with the people who are going to make the strategy happen in practice.

Sources

- *The Discipline of Market Leaders: choose your customers, narrow your focus, dominate your market*, Michael Treacy and Fred Wiersema, Perseus Books, 1995
- 'Leading change: why transformation efforts fail', Professor John Kotter, *Harvard Business Review*, January 2007
- 'Turning Great Strategy into Performance'. Michael C Mankins and Richard Steele, Maradon, *Harvard Business Review*, July-August 2005
- *Are you having difficulties in the implementation of strategy and change, it could all be about leadership*' MCE paper, January 2011

Growth
Employee experience
Innovation
Diversity and inclusion
Partnerships
Inspiration

LEADER'S
DRIVERS

Customer focus

Digitalization

Process

Brands

Effectiveness

Strategy execution
Personalization

6.

LEADERSHIP FOR
EFFECTIVENESS

What makes for effective leaders? It's not just about vision. It's about achieving results. Too often we see compelling appointments to senior posts who fall short of expectations, sometimes putting organizations at risk of failure.

You can be the most engaging, authentic and emotionally intelligent leader, but it won't drive the results on which an organization ultimately depends. Of course, it matters what you want to be. It equally matters what you have to do.

When talking to organizations struggling to perform, Johan Beeckmans, a senior associate of MCE with long experience of managing change, always asks executives a series of questions. 'Many believe that if they have a mission, a vision and a set of values, they have a strategy. That's not the case and it's why they find themselves making so many mistakes.'

'First, be clear about what your business is about and how it competes. Then ask yourself five questions: what's the purpose of being in your market? what are you looking to achieve? who are your target customers? what is the value you offer them? and what capabilities are required to fulfil their expectations?'

Failure to answer any of those questions satisfactorily spells trouble. Even the most august organizations can lose their way, however well led they may seem to be. At turning points, such as turnarounds or transformations, as we shall see, these questions come more sharply into focus. You can't rely on reputations to get by. Your future as an organization is going to depend on making sure you have the right leaders in the right place to drive effectiveness and align teams.

Core competencies

In the view one of America's most admired chief executives, A.G. Lafley, who revitalised Procter & Gamble in the 2000s, strategies are regularly flawed. In a conversation with *Forbes* in 2013, he commented that many of those in charge are 'trying to be all things to all people, they're not really making choices: where are they going to play and, as importantly, where are they not going to play? what is winning? what are their core capabilities and competencies? and how are they going to measure progress?'.

For Lafley, there are two timeless fundamentals to business strategy. 'One part is how do you position yourself versus the other choices the customer has in the market. In our model, we call those choices where to play and how to win. The other part is what are the capabilities that make you different, better and more competitive. We talked about those as core competencies at P&G.'

Lafley made 'a straightforward definition' of five core competencies: for P&G, which you will probably recognise as parallel to our model:

- deeper understanding of consumers;

- innovation leader in household and personal care;

- brand leader, building those we already had and creating new ones;

- the ability to partner with our customers, suppliers and other innovators;

- and finally, the ability to scale our learning on a global basis.

'They were decisive in our industry. They distinguished us when we really did them well.'

The billion dollar turnaround

So how do you become more effective when the pressure is on to perform? How, for instance, do you turn seven underperforming business units with $450 million in debt into an independently listed company that had $475 million in reserves and bought back $200 million of its own shares?

It was a task that William Monahan faced as the new chief executive of Imation, a spin-out from 3M of its non-core data imaging and data operations. If these businesses were ever to make money again, he says in his book *Billion Dollar Turnaround*, a 'wrenching transformation' was required to find a new business model.

At launch the new business, Imation, had $2.4 billion in sales, but was competing on price with formidable competitors, had a dispirited workforce, unsettled customers and investors who were ready to sell.

In such a tight, uncertain business, says Monahan, it's hard to leave the office with a smile on your face. 'But I quickly learned, you'd darn well better or you create so much uncertainty, it can be very harmful.'

'If you take on an attitude of gloom and doom, that attitude will set a negative tone. This a huge factor in turnarounds and start-ups. The attitude of the leaders creates the attitude of the employees.'

'Sometimes leaders must be moved out because they are unable to exude a positive attitude. Optimism is critical to a turnaround. The situation may look dire, the mountain may look insurmountable, you may be weary, but there is no option. In order to survive, you must reach the goals you've set.'

It's a lesson he learnt from one of the enduring classics of American management writing, Napoleon Hill's *Think and Grow Rich*. 'A management team with a common purpose and a positive attitude can be compared to a number of storage batteries hooked up in a series, instead of each one standing alone. The output is greatly magnified because they are linked. What you can't afford is a dead cell siphoning off power or shorting the group.'

As a leader, says Monahan, 'you must search out the positive people on your team, the optimists, and support that optimism and their courage in facing difficult situations ... leadership must be positive about the ability to change, improve and eventually win'.

'People are a company's most vital asset, but you can have too many people and you can have the wrong people. Those who are committed deserve leadership that is willing to step forward and make the changes necessary to insure everyone is productive and contributing.'

The right leaders

So how do you go about making sure you have the right leaders in place? For Johan Beeckmans, it was a question he was asked to resolve while he was at a company transforming itself from a commodity producer into a higher value innovator. What were the competencies required to fulfil this ambition?

Based on interviews with the executives themselves and industry surveys, Beeckmans identified ten competencies in three categories:

- **Executive savvy**: engaging others, global mindset, gaining commitment.

- **Creating value:** strategic insight, acting with foresight, leveraging relationships, driving for excellence.

- **Making it happen**: leading others, holding people accountable, building a sustainable organization.

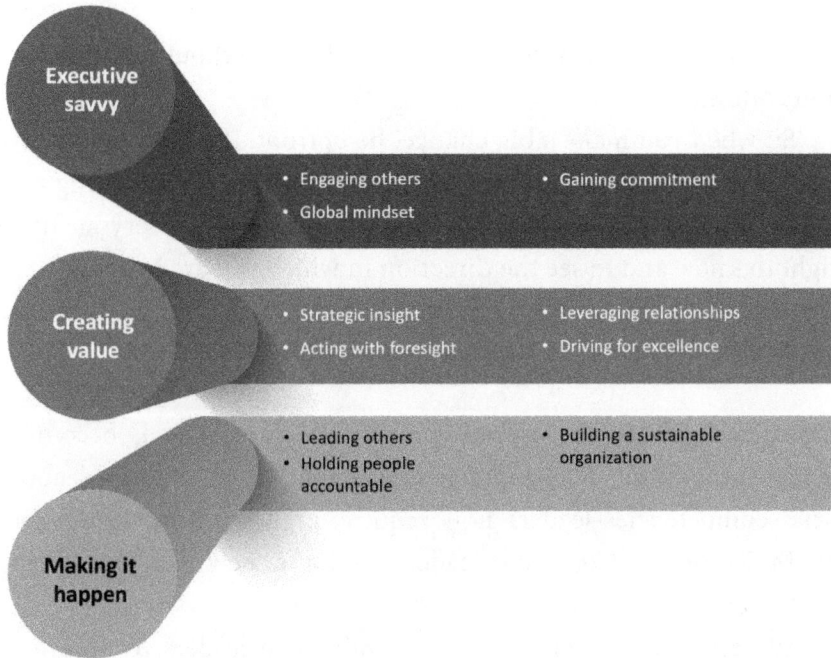

Executive savvy
- Engaging others   - Gaining commitment
- Global mindset

Creating value
- Strategic insight   - Leveraging relationships
- Acting with foresight   - Driving for excellence

- Leading others   - Building a sustainable
- Holding people   organization
  accountable

Making it happen

Figure 1: ten competencies for effective leadership (source: MCE)

The results revealed three types of leader: those with the potential already, those who could develop it and those who would never make it. Such differences became particularly stark when focused on the innovative direction in which the company wished to travel.

It led to some difficult decisions. One leader of a unit, revered by all, never made his figures. He was replaced by someone with the potential to develop as a leader who had the unit back in profit within eight months.

The company started to recruit based on Beeckmans' ten competencies. 'We immediately saw the difference,' he says. 'In two years, this spirit of innovation had taken it from the middle of the pack to one of the industry leaders.'

Such a change in mindset takes two to three years, says Beeckmans. Even then, it'll be in the balance without commitment and communication.

'So when you make a big change, be upfront. If a senior executive no longer fits the role, explain why. Don't say they are pursuing new opportunities or spending more time with the family. Everyone has a right to know and to see the direction in which you are heading.'

Shifts in mindset

Organizations are themselves now being transformed, becoming more open, fluid and adaptable, changing the assumptions about what competencies leaders now require, argues a May 2023 paper by McKinsey & Co, 'New leadership for a new era of thriving organizations'.

'We are moving from an era of individual leaders to an era of networked leadership teams that steer the organization,' it says. 'The old hierarchical model of leadership is increasingly seen as an obstacle to meeting the complex demands facing today's organizations.'

'This new approach calls on leaders to make fundamental evolutionary shifts, well beyond the standard expectation that they continually develop additional skills. They must in fact reimagine themselves.'

McKinsey identifies five shifts in mindset they must make, going beyond their traditional skills:

- **From profit to impact**: as managers, they have delivered profits to shareholders with a mindset of preservation; as visionaries, they will generate holistic impact for all stakeholders with a mindset of possibility.

- **Architects of value**: as planners, they have competed for existing value through advantage with a mindset of scarcity; as architects, they will co-create new value through reimagining with a mindset of abundance.

- **From directors to partners**: as directors, they have commanded through structured hierarchies with a mindset of authority; as catalysts, they will collaborate in empowered networks with a mindset of partnership.

- **Coaches for rapid learning**: as controllers, they have administered through detailed prediction with a mindset of certainty; as coaches, they will evolve through rapid learning with a mindset of discovery.

- **Whole humans**: as professionals, they have met expectations with a mindset of conformity; as humans, they are their whole best selves with a mindset of authenticity.

Historically, says McKinsey, we are at a moment when mental and emotional barriers are breaking down. 'We are already seeing some organizations evolve and transform to meet the demands for sustainable, inclusive growth. More and more companies will follow their lead.'

Bold and responsible

The challenge is to replace old models of leadership and think about the future differently, says MCE in its flagship programme for executive development. Uniformity and control are being replaced by creativity and speed. How can you inspire your people to respond with imagination and agility?

For leaders, MCE says, it's about being both bold and responsible. When their hardest challenge is to have the mental flexibility to respond to transitions and transformations, their social intelligence is at a premium in creating a culture that inspires innovation and high performance. As effective leaders, all their interactions count in building the confidence to take their organizations and their people beyond expectations.

Leadership drives efficiency in all you do, so people really care, reflecting and improving on what they do. Such operational excellence, of course, then has a wider impact on your business and its relationships with customers.

Illustration: leading for results at APK Group

APK Group designs, builds and maintains smart, sustainable cities with roads, energy, telecoms and water. Still a family business, it is growing at 20 percent a year and aims to double in size every five years. Currently, APK's revenues are €475 million and it has 2250 employees.

It's a compelling proposition to act as a one-stop shop, says Martin Broens, the chief executive. 'We can put it in all the services in the last mile at once. For vehicle charging points, for instance, it's a big advantage when all the details are within our own capabilities.'

As a business, APK is flat in structure. 'We want all our employees to feel ownership. It's in our DNA. We are highly results driven. We have no pyramids here. We are not limiting anyone in a narrow space. Like football, you can play all over the field. With lean, efficient procedures and a set of firm ground rules, we can stimulate entrepreneurship without falling into bureaucracy. If we're going to grow at 20 percent a year, we can't be too rigid. We need to be entrepreneurs in getting things done.'

'These entrepreneurial values are very important for us in the recruitment process. The values, culture and way of work in a family business are different from those in a multinational. We want to recruit those who share our entrepreneurial values.'

Progress is measured by everyone having their own set of key performance indicators. The foremen are responsible for the efficiency and safety of a job. For project leaders, profitability is added. Then for the management board, the metrics are quarterly growth and return on capital.

These targets drill down right into the company. Everyone can see progress every month. Then at the end of the year, they are all asked whether they can stretch their targets any further. 'We calculate it together, then we challenge it, but it remains a personal goal for you to achieve,' says Broens.

'As a leader, you have to be out there. You really have to get out a clear message. It's about showing a direction and inspiring people to find their own way. You have to take them with you because they are the ones executing the strategy.'

Conclusion

Leaders have then the responsibility to structure the environment, the internal processes, the way managers think towards effectiveness at any price. It has to be a shared value, a shared goal.

Leaders will guide teams to what such effectiveness really means. Otherwise it is too open to interpretation. Leadership for effectiveness drives the whole organization towards a precise mentality, a clear focus. It is about making choices. If you are going to reach for the ultimate levels of performance, you can't be too broad.

Sources

- A.G. Lafley defines effective business strategy, interview with *Forbes*, 2013: https://youtu.be/FlurK3LeTpg
- *Billion Dollar Turnaround: the 3M spin-off that became Imation*, William T Monahan, Oaklea Press, 2005
- 'New leadership for a new era of thriving organizations', Aaron de Smet, Arne Gast, Johanne Lavoie and Michael Lurie, *McKinsey Quarterly*, May 2023

The circular diagram shows "LEADER'S DRIVERS" at the center, surrounded by segments labeled: Growth, Employee experience, Diversity and inclusion, Inspiration, Customer focus, Brands, Personalization, Strategy execution, Effectiveness, Digitalization, Partnerships, Innovation. Inner ring labels: Business, People, Market, Process.

7.

LEADERSHIP FOR DIGITALIZATION

All organizations are becoming more digital. However, many are misdirecting their efforts and wasting millions of euros. It is only a few who fully appreciate how far-reaching the implications are for how they operate and what they offer.

'Digital transformation is the fundamental rewiring of how an organization operates,' says McKinsey & Co in a new book, *Rewired* (Wiley, 2023). 'Digital transformations hinge less on how companies *use* digital and more on how they *become* digital.'

The mistake that many organizations make is to become distracted by the latest technology, then try to apply it to existing products and structures. A prime example was the British government. In 2010, it found itself hosting thousands of disconnected websites and relying on a narrow base of suppliers. It consolidated all its services onto one website and opened up its tendering to many more bidders. By 2015, it had radically simplified its service for users and saved itself £4 billion a year.

'Faced with the digital revolution, many people in large organizations instinctively see its consequences as another layer of complexity,' say four veterans of the British government's digital service who wrote a book about their experience, *Digital Transformation at Scale* (Greenway, Terrett, Bracken and Loosemore, LPP, 2018).

'Digital is not a new function,' they say. 'It is not even a new way of running the existing functions of an organization. It is a new way of running organizations. A successful digital transformation makes it possible not only to deliver products and services that are simpler, cheaper and better, but for the organization as a whole to operate effectively in the online era.'

So why is such simplicity so hard to achieve? According to an article in the *Harvard Business Review* (Edelman and Abraham, April 2022), it is only 10 percent down to technology and 20 percent to data. The remaining 70 percent is about people and how you run your organization via processes and targets. In other words, the direction you set as a leader and the interventions you make have a profound impact on how everyone now interacts with your organization.

'You can't start from a narrow technology point of view,' says William Mulhern on the MCE faculty, who spent 20 years in regional and global sales at Cisco. 'That way you'll quickly run into problems. As the leader, you're leveraging expertise from across the organization.'

'At the same time, you can't assume the technical team will do what you think. You have to be savvy enough to hold them to account.'

Digital experiences

Let's take a look at how contrasting digital experiences can be. I was recently flying with a low-cost airline that prides itself on its digitalization. I wanted to switch my booking. At check-in, the screen told me the cost was €8. I made the change and was charged €56. I complained to an agent, who referred me to the web, which didn't recognise what I was saying, because it fell outside the programmed range of scenarios.

As a next step, you can then try to call the option menu. After many attempts to make your point, you are told that you are bypassing the system and you are invited you make a new reservation. At which point, you abandon your complaint. The airline might have made an extra €48 off me this time, but it has lost my goodwill and, no doubt, many others like me.

It's a choice, and sometimes a highly profitable one, to focus on digitalization in this way, rather than customers or employees, so we cannot judge. When poorly led, digitalization risks such disappointments at the point of use and can have a longer term impact on performance. When properly led, however, it can transform the efficiency and profitability of what might be viewed as a legacy business. It's about finding a way digitally to align with your customer's expectations.

During lockdown, Ikea took on the challenge of accelerating its digital capabilities in selling home goods. Three-quarters of its stores had to close and its customers were migrating online. In three years to 2021, it tripled online sales to 30 percent of total revenue.

In an interview with the *Harvard Business Review* (June 2021), the Google veteran that Ikea recruited as its chief digital officer, Barbara Martin Coppola, talked about how to sustain a culture as distinctive as Ikea's while changing almost everything.

First, Ikea has learnt to operate at two speeds while operating from one space: first for retail during opening hours and then for ecommerce 24/7. Goods can be delivered from anywhere in the supply chain. Data and analytics support how decisions are made.

However, the digital transformation for her is about more than technology. 'We are exploring new offers to our customers, new ways to bring our offers to customers and new ways to operate our business. To be successful, digital needs to be embedded in every aspect of Ikea. Digital is a way of working, making decisions and managing the company.'

'At the top of the iceberg, we revamp everything around customer interaction and new purchasing journeys. Under the surface, we are making huge changes to our business and operating model.'

Data, analytics and process

Data will start determining more of your decisions and actions. However, without a system in place, its value will be limited. So your first step is to have a clear sense of who you are, where you are going and how you want to organize your data, says MCE's Mulhern. 'It's hard work, but it will pay off in future.'

Your aim is to create an architecture that everyone can access. Once you have a clear model, you can start using analytics to give you insights, make predictions and map out probabilities.

To gain efficiencies, however, depends on your understanding of all the different processes involved, says Mulhern. 'During lockdown, you could rely on force of will to get things done. However, it's hard to keep your head above the water when you're making a bet on the future and you're not quite sure how your business functions.'

'Transformation gives you a more solid footing. You will know what your capabilities are and where your strengths are. It all comes together and allows you to do more.'

Cross-functional teams

Digitalization is not about a single use, such as customer calls, but about the whole process of a customer journey. So it's a complex puzzle which demands input from different parts of the organization. 'You're not going to get anywhere by letting people go off independently and figure out what they are going to do,' says Mulhern. 'You have to bring in all the subject experts and give them the responsibility for figuring it out together.'

It also means making sure they have the power and authority to move forward. It's one of the two big reasons why digital transformations fail, says an article by Accenture in the *Harvard Business Review* (October 2019). 'If top managers aren't on the same page, it makes it difficult for direct reports to agree on what to prioritise and how to measure progress.'

So before you make an investment, says Accenture, 'define and articulate how the company will the build the organization around the desired solutions'.

Four starting points

Transformation can take a number of forms. Without clarity about which one you are pursuing, leaders can feel themselves pulled in different directions, says an article in *Harvard Business Review* (Furr, Shipilov, Rouillard and Hermon-Laurens, January 2022).

Too often the wrong people are put in charge with the wrong resources and the wrong targets. Instead, digital transformation is better seen as multi-faceted, says the *HBR* article, which can have differing goals depending on your industry and your digital maturity. Essentially, it happens in one of four ways, each of which will be led and resourced differently:

- **IT uplift**: upgrade the digital infrastructure with up-to-date tools under the direction of the chief technology officer.

- **Digitizing operations**: optimise existing processes to streamline business growth under the direction of the chief finance officer or chief operating officer.

- **Digital marketing**: use digital tools to interact with customers and make sales under the direction of the chief marketing officer.

- **New ventures**: create new business models, new products or new services under the direction of the chief executive or head of sales.

The outcomes for each type of transformation will significantly improve, says *HBR*, when you have the right leader, the rights measures and the right targets in place.

Start small

If you're a new venture, you can usually find all your digital tools off the shelf. You are less bound by existing norms and you are free to focus on how to meet users' expectations. Existing services, however, always come with baggage. Choices have already been made, behaviours are set.

'If possible, start with small services that are completely new or so irretrievably broken that you have a completely blank sheet of paper to work with,' say the authors of *Digital Transformation at Scale*. 'After a point, there is no avoiding your brownfield (or legacy) services. To become a digital organization, you have to fix them or close them.'

Design principles

In the transformation of the British government's services, a set of design principles was distributed about how digital was going to be delivered. They weren't written as a strategy from the top. They were the result of the digital team's experience of managing the first projects.

They were deliberately pragmatic, giving a signal to civil servants about how control and responsibility for outcomes was being taken back into the organization. Later endorsed by the World Bank and adopted by many other countries, the ten principles were:

- Start with user needs.

- Do less.

- Design with data.

- Do the hard work to make it simple.

- Iterate, then iterate again.

- This is for everyone.

- Understand context.

- Build digital services, not websites.

- Be consistent, not uniform.

- Makes things open, it makes things better.

For the government's digital service, it represented a start in building a new culture, but it also came with a warning. 'The reality of delivering this kind of culture change in a large organization is invariably messier than those clean messages.'

Pilot to scale

The second big reason that digital transformations fail, says Accenture, is the divide between the digital capabilities to support the pilot and those to scale it. 'When this problem isn't addressed, companies may face a choice between accepting long delays in ramping up production or attempts by leadership at rapid, unwieldy change to fulfil what they have promised.'

Either you look outside to close the gaps: for instance, by building an ecosystem of experts and start-ups. Or you establish innovation factories that put organizational muscle behind digital re-invention. 'They are not limited to R&D or product design. Instead, they work end to end, starting with the incubation of new ideas, moving through the design of potential solutions, then on to deployment and scaling. They're highly integrated into the organization, including people from all functions, not just R&D.'

Digitalizing with humans

Digitalization is not just about changing working practices, but mindsets too. As we saw during the pandemic, if digitalization is rushed, it leads to disengagement and people leaving. So human resources is itself under review. For 20 years, it has been about creating an employee experience that attracts and retains people. Now it is becoming a wider question of human connection and people sustainability.

HR left its transactional roots long ago to become more transformational. For digitalization, it is taking a step further. It is now an optimiser of human capital, says Helena Stucky de Quay, an MCE associate who specialises in digital learning and upgrading HR systems. 'HR is not just a business partner,' she says, 'it is becoming a human partner, driving connections across the organization.'

This shift in emphasis towards managing the human experience of digitalization presents three distinct challenges for HR: readying everyone to transform; adapting how decisions are made; and equipping itself with new skills.

'Digital and AI keep redefining what is expected of the workforce. You can be ahead one day, but behind the next. So you have to learn and unlearn constantly. This agility has become a competence that everyone now requires.'

'As an organization, you are then looking to design systems for making the right decisions and adopting policies that allow you to collect data about your people while maintaining their trust. Regimes vary in how restrictive or permissive they are, which can complicate how you target talent, for instance.'

'Many of the processes that once occupied HR, such as finding and screening talent, are now being taken over by digital and AI. Employees can also manage most of the details of their own packages. So HR finds itself fulfilling a wider role in helping employees adapt to change that requires a new mindset as a human partner, not just a business partner.'

Illustration: digital as a disruptor
Statement from Jean-Charles Samuelian-Werve, co-founder and chief executive of Alan

'Our mission at Alan is to empower everyone to live a longer, healthier life. Our goal is to extend the quality years of life expectancy for everyone. It is an ambitious mission that has driven me since I was a teenager. Science already shows that prevention and timely access to the right care adds eight to ten years of life expectancy. People have been lost in a complex healthcare system for too long.'

'It's our job to make healthcare and prevention easy to navigate and even fun to use. We are building the one-stop health partner: we seamlessly integrate insurance coverage, prevention and access to care.'

'The competition is taking note. As we continue to innovate and grow, we're seeing traditional insurers starting to invest in digital capabilities and user experience, even if it is hard for them to change their back-end and infrastructure. However, our unique approach to health and wellness, coupled with our comprehensive services, sets us apart. We push everyday to be leading the way in the industry.'

As a company created from scratch, digital has always been inherent in Alan's culture. 'Every Alaner is an owner and makes decisions on their own on behalf of the whole company. Our teams are encouraged to challenge the norm and leverage technology to improve the experience of customers and members. Through our culture of leadership by context and example, the digital focus naturally cascades to every Alaner, because it is all they witness everyday.'

Alan has no set style of how to manage. 'Each company finds its own way to achieve its own type of greatness. On our side, we value autonomy, innovation, adaptability and radical transparency. Our written culture is a key asset. It's our knowledge bank, a powerful tool that fuels our performance and sets us apart. Our teams are empowered to make decisions, experiment with new ideas and learn from failures. We focus on results more than traditional hierarchical structures.'

Of course, Alan has experienced some resistance. 'If it wasn't hard, other companies would have done what we do. We take joy in the hurdles, in the challenges, that are opportunities to make something differentiated, new. We cope by staying true to our core values and leadership principles. We remain focused on the journey and the mission.'

Conclusion

A focus as relentless as Samuelian-Werve's is what all leaders require if they are to fulfil their ambitions of becoming digital. In banking, for instance, that resolve was tested by the transformation of the workplace during the pandemic. Many in the industry are now expressing doubts about the culture of allowing employees to work from home.

ING, by contrast, has stuck to its ambition, first expressed in 2015, to become one of the first and biggest digital banks, promising customers to make services digitally available anytime and anywhere, however much circumstances have changed since then.

'Our ambition to keep transforming into a leading data-driven digital bank remains firms', its chief executive, Steven van Rijswijk told *Fintech Magazine* in 2020. 'However, the challenging external environment requires that we remain flexible in how and where we deliver our Think Forward strategy.'

That determination is reflected in the culture that it is creating. Its competitors might have their doubts about hybrid working. In 2021, ING's then global head of talent management, Christophe Vanden Eede, told *Unleash*: 'empowerment is in our DNA, making sure that people are allowed to find the best possible way for them to work.'

'We really do believe that hybrid working can bring benefits in employee wellbeing and engagement. If you have happier employees, they will make sure your customers become happy, which normally translates into a happy profit. So it is a win, win, win.'

Sources

- 'Customer Experience in the age of AI', David C. Edelman and Mark Abraham, *Harvard Business Review*, March/April 2022
- *Rewired: a McKinsey guide to outcompeting in the age of digital and AI*, Wiley, 2023
- 'What is digital transformation?', McKinsey & Co, June 2023
- *Digital Transformation at Scale: Why the strategy is delivery*, Andrew Greenaway, Ben Terrett, Mike Bracken and Tom Loosemore, London Publishing Partnership, 2018
- 'Inside Ikea's digital transformation', Thomas Stackpole, *Harvard Business Review*, June 2021
- 'The two big reason that digital transformations fail', Mike Sutcliff, Raghav Narsaly and Aarohi Sen, Accenture, *Harvard Business Review*, October 2019
- 'The four pillars of successful digital transformation', Nathan Furr, Andrew Shipilov, Didier Rouillard and Antoine Hermon-Laurens, *Harvard Business Review*, January 2022
- 'The essential components of digital transformation', Tomas Chamorro-Premuzic, chief innovation office at Manpower, *Harvard Business Review*, November 21

PART 3

PEOPLE

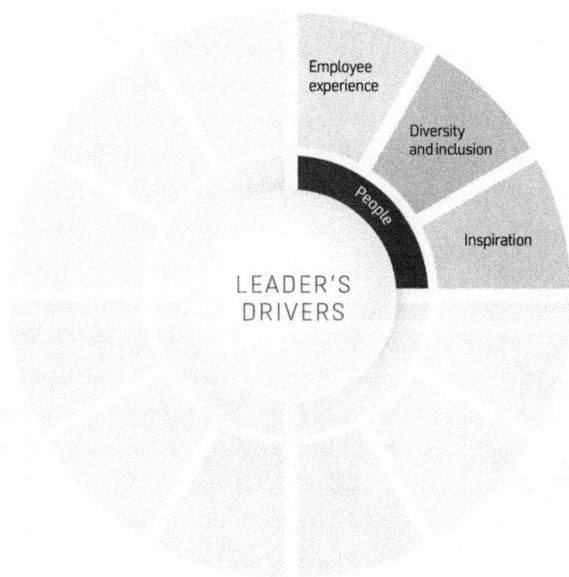

Employee
experience

Growth

Innovation

Diversity
and inclusion

Partnerships

People

Inspiration

LEADER'S
DRIVERS

Digitalization

Customer
focus

Effectiveness

Brands

Strategy
execution

Personalization

8.

LEADERSHIP FOR
EMPLOYEE EXPERIENCE

At a global distributor in Sweden, employees typically stay in their posts for more than ten years. In many other workplaces, particularly following the pandemic, the figure is much lower, sometimes just over a year. It's a gap that represents wasted efforts in recruitment, disappointed expectations, a lack of energy, inconsistent customer service and low productivity. So how do these Swedes do it better?

First, they have a head of employee experience on the senior team, ready to argue for a more supportive – and enjoyable – workplace. Second, they have a clear proposition for their employees: we will help to make you financially independent. Then they insist on putting the human first in any interactions: if someone is having a bad day, it's fine to say so.

The principle is that everyone is there to help each other. Meetings spend less time reviewing the latest figures and more time on finding out how everyone is feeling. No judgments are made. Any shortcomings or failures are treated as opportunities to learn. That way everyone has the freedom to speak their mind and be themselves.

Organizations with such engaged workforces are at a significant advantage. More effort. More time. More ideas. More recommending you. It's a virtuous circle that many aspire to replicate.

In the absence of a distinctive culture inspired by a founding team, however, many are struggling to come anywhere close. Levels of engagement fell steadily in the 2010s before taking a harder knock in the pandemic, when pressures in the workplace led to a wave of burn-outs and resignations.

For leaders, it demands a rethink about how they are defining employee experience. They know, says Alain Thys, a senior associate at MCE and an experience architect at FutureLab, that they have little chance of making any strategic transformations unless 'all their people are on the bus'.

It isn't enough anymore to track engagement and make one-off initiatives to improve it. Instead, it's about reviewing the fundamentals of an employee's experience with you: the key moments in your relationship, a sense of purpose, communications that speak to the heart, an environment to support performance and the right flow of live data.

Human resources can influence these outcomes, of course, but it is up to leaders to create the framework. The calculation is that if you start to get all these elements right for the long term, engagement in the short term will follow, as it does instinctively at the Swedish global distributor. So let's look at what choices, leaders can make in putting employee experience at the heart of their strategy.

A more human deal

The transactional model on which organizations have relied for so long is losing its appeal. Competitive pay and an attractive package of benefits are no longer enough. For the current generation of talent, a sense of belonging and coherence matter too.

In a report for the *Harvard Business Review* in the Spring of 2022, Gartner's HR practice observed that a change of emphasis is required towards 'a human deal that makes employees feel cared for financially, physically and emotionally'.

Less than a third of workers were found to feel their organizations offer anything special and nearly half were experiencing more stress than ever before. Such shortcomings were exposed during the pandemic, leading many to step back from the workplace altogether during the so-called 'great resignation', when they realised they weren't in the right place to fulfil themselves.

Once, not too much would be asked about employees' lives outside work. Now, Gartner reports, expectations are different: employees expect to be treated as whole individuals and to feel deeply connected to their organization. 'They want their managers to know about their personal commitments and make accommodations where possible.'

It goes well beyond allowing more remote working. Instead, it demands a 'radical flexibility' in allowing employees to determine how they are going to work, which Gartner has found can raise the number of high-performing employees by 40 percent.

Design thinking

It is a profound shift from a traditional hierarchy to a more flexible, responsive model. In a report on the 'new possible' in the workplace in September 2021, McKinsey & Co describes it as an approach in which 'organizations work together with their people to create personalized, authentic and motivating experiences that strengthen individual, team and company performance'.

Let me give you a personal example of what that means. As a student, I started work at an immersive language training company. The owner summed up his approach as a 'fresh flower in every room'. He wanted each student to know when they arrived that it had been cut for them. In the same way, we now want to put employees at the centre of their experience with you, their employer.

By endeavouring to give them this kind of experience, you will follow each touchpoint of their relationship with you: when they are recruited, when they join, how they learn, how they progress, when they leave. Each of these points is an opportunity for you, as their employer, to have a cut-flower moment and dazzle. It will have lasting consequences for how engaged your employees become, how motivated they are, how well they perform and whether they would recommend you to their friends.

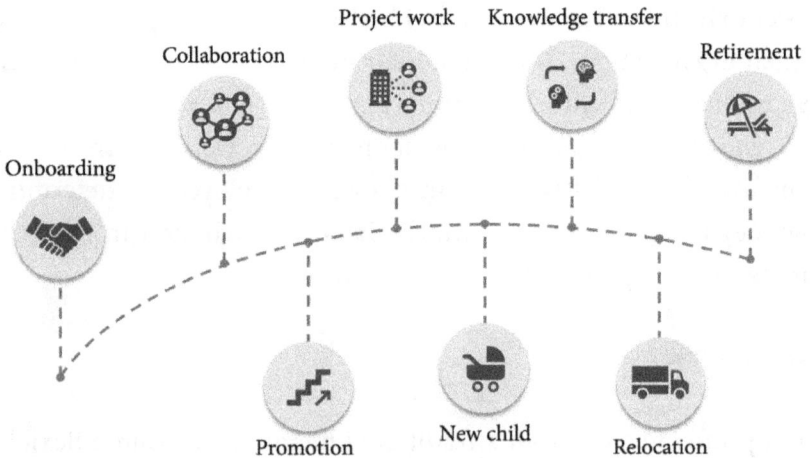

Figure 1: key employee experiences enabled by a better designed digital workplace (source: Gallup)

For McKinsey, this new possible means adopting the fundamentals of design thinking. 'You put your workers first by exploring and responding to how they view their employee journeys, then delivering tailored interventions that focus on critical moments that matter to maximise satisfaction, performance and productivity. In doing so, organizations can become more inspiring, collaborative and centred on creating an experience that is meaningful and enjoyable'.

The answer is rarely more pay, reports McKinsey: 'employees want a powerful sense of agency – being able to influence outcomes that matter to them – allied with a strong sense of identity and belonging'.

Creating an employee experience

Employees not want to feel as if they are having a great customer experience. If the destination is clear, the path is less so. In January 2022, in a commentary about the great resignation of employees following the pandemic, McKinsey found that more half of those who quit in the last six months of 2021 did not feel valued by their organizations (54 percent) or their manager (52 percent). Or they lacked a sense of belonging (51 percent).

Like many of us, I know how tough it is, despite all your best intentions. We recently recruited a highly competent project manager in her thirties, who we hoped could end up heading a team. Yet she resigned at the first real hurdle she encountered, because she got an instruction that was different from what she had expected to do when contacting a client.

So how can you start to create a more positive employee experience? On our programmes at MCE, we follow a three-step programme:

- Clarify your vision about what matters to your employees, then draw up and validate a set of employee experience standards that aligns behaviour to your values.

- Plan a roadmap, establishing where you currently stand. Get buy-in from all your leaders and set out the outcomes, actions and targets you expect.

- Implement a programme to embed employee experience into your culture, tracking progress and highlighting wins.

Figure 2: a three-step programme to a more positive employee experience (source: MCE)

Such an approach goes far beyond one-off initiatives to lift your employees' mood in the short term. It's an integrated strategy for aligning expectations and behaviours throughout the company.

Purposive employees

In today's workplace, employees are expecting their work to give them a significant sense of purpose. When it's lacking or when it's brought into question, as we have seen following the pandemic, talent starts to migrate.

On the upside, according to a McKinsey paper, 'Help your employees find purpose' (April 2021), if 70 percent of employees are finding their purpose at work, it represents significant potential if you can align a purposive workforce with your organization.

Variations occur within the headline figure: a sense of purpose is felt most strongly by senior executives and less on the frontline. So, as a starting point, the paper recommends, it pays to help employees find more personal meaning in their day-to-day work. As well as feeling more engaged, they will try harder and innovate more.

Expectations are also rising for leaders to express a clearly defined sense of purpose for their organizations, although it's easy to misjudge your response, says an article in the *Harvard Business Review*, 'What is the purpose of your purpose?' (March/April 2022). Any inconsistencies are a sure way to disengaging employees, as well as customers, communities and investors.

Ideally, a purpose should be authentic, relevant and practical. The difficulty is that it can be expressed in one of three ways: cause (the good you support), culture (your intent) and competence (your function). In defining your purpose, it's about more than marketing and communications. Yes, you have to appeal to your market, but you equally have to engage your employees and manage your risks.

A passionate chief executive with a cause can elevate an otherwise mundane business. However, says the *HBR* paper, employees often respond better to a more low-key statement based on culture or competence.

As a leader, you want to be sure to create a blend that inspires all your different audiences without raising false expectations. As well as taking a top-down view to bring all the elements of the business together, you have to remember that purpose will be largely experienced from the bottom-up.

Strategic transformations

In this respect, we could all learn from the US army, says Alain Thys. It insists that its officers understand the values of those under their command. That way, when in a high-pressure situation, orders can be given in a way that takes emotional account of what everyone cares about. So they're not being ordered into action on the authority of the president, but on what they all value as a team.

It's worth following the same principle for strategic transformations within organizations, he says. 'Otherwise progress will slow. Your people won't be getting up early to shift a key performance indicator or to make more profit.'

Such was the case for the Dutch insurer, ING. Strategically, it wanted to improve its net promoter score (or those who would recommend it to family and friends), a highly influential metric in winning new business. However, as a term, it only meant anything much to a couple of people in the head office. For the 10,000 people in the field, it was neither here nor there.

So like a US army officer or a design thinker, ING paused to consider what its employees actually cared about. As colleagues, it turned out that they were looking out for each other to an unusual degree. So the campaign to improve the net promoter score was framed as an emotional video about what it meant to care for someone and why ING cared for its customers.

It spread like wildfire, recalls Thys. 'It wasn't a management message. It was the employees' values. For the management team, it was a big ask to let go of their KPIs and go with emotion. It might not always work, but its impact has been to make ING number one in all its markets, except one.'

Able to perform

Your talent might now be willing and ready to engage. Without the right environment, however, they won't be able to perform. If their workplace isn't conducive to what you are asking them to do, then it's a short step towards even the most enthusiastic employees disengaging or burning out.

Before the pandemic, many leaders were thinking about how to redesign their workplaces to encourage people to collaborate and create more. Now leaders have to let go of all the orthodoxies about how they think work happens. It's time to design from the ground up again.

First, it's best to be clear about what behaviours your customers require. Then it's a question of creating an environment to support people wherever they are: at home, at the airport, on the road or at a client.

So one supplier, for instance, decided to consolidate all its account handling for large industrials. In principle, it made sense. In practice, the new system was almost impossible to use. When everyone was together in the office, it was easier to exercise control and pick up problems. Now everything is much more fragmented.

Leaders can easily fall into the trap of making assumptions based on their own perspective. No doubt, they have a well-equipped, well-supported office of their own at home. Those dealing with customers on the frontline may well find it more of a struggle. So it makes sense to make sure that new systems for managing accounts, for instance, are as easy to use as possible. Of if you expect people to work from the airport, then give them access to the lounges.

Another possibility when problems occur is to have a leader available on the spot to help employees resolve them and make difficult decisions. It's almost as if they were sitting in reception ready to back anyone up. Such conversations with a leader are fundamental to employees experience and are what many most miss about not being close enough to bump into each other in the workplace.

When leaders are designing future environments for their organizations and support for their employees, it's worth being clear about such feelings. What really brings them into work? For many it is social. Some want to learn. Others want to escape cramped conditions at home. All these will play a part in creating an environment that lets your employees perform at their best.

Metrics

As you design your employees' experience, you will want to keep close track of progress. Here again, you may well want to keep an open mind about how you go about collecting data. Old orthodoxies may no longer apply in taking account of how you are managing your talent.

Organizations can continue paying up to $250,000 for an annual employee survey. However, many now question whether they are too top down. The same questions are often asked year after year. Answers vary by a percentage point or two.

An alternative is to learn from consumer marketing. No one conducts customer satisfaction surveys anymore. Instead, they learn from each touchpoint.

So you listen to what your employees are saying to you. You ask simpler, more open questions, encouraging people to say what they think, rather than just ticking a box. You take back their answers, prototype them and see if they work. In that way, you will learn what your talent really values and you are then in a better position to compete for the best skills.

In this context, annual appraisals can be another source of anguish. They can take up too much time and lag behind what skills you require, often turning into negotiations about compensation, instead of discussions about performance.

Instead, regular check-ins based on live data work better. You can pick up what is working, what is falling behind and what is going to happen next. For leaders, it will mean improving their skills in holding the candid conversations that many of them prefer to avoid.

An experimental alternative source of live data is to use smartwatches to track your employees' level of immersion (with their permission, of course, and respecting their privacy). In aggregate, you will be able to see how safe they are feeling and how happy they are.

Such techniques are already proving popular with those in highly stressful working conditions, such as nurses in emergency wards, picking up signs of a burn-out two days before it happens.

Illustration: employees creating their own experience at Calida

Calida is an international group of four fashion brands in lingerie, nightwear, underwear and outdoor furniture in Switzerland, Germany, France and the Unites States. The reactions of its employees to the transformation of the workplace have varied. Everyone goes into the office at its French fashion brand next to the Louvre in the centre of Paris. Barely anyone puts in an appearance at its ecommerce team in Germany.

'If you were to say that you would expect everyone to be there three days a week, you could lose 30 to 40 percent of them,' says Felix Sulzberger, the chair of the group, now acting as chief executive again. 'The workplace changed more in those two Covid years than in all my time before.'

'You can't manage with rules any more,' he says. 'You can only manage your culture. For us, it's a challenge because the cultures vary so much across our four brands.'

Originally, Sulzberger was responsible for updating Calida from an old-fashioned maker of nightwear, whose pyjamas appeared in every German and Swiss child's stocking at Christmas. Today its four brands, Aubade, Lafuma Mobilier, Calida and Cosabella, have combined sales of €330 million a year and employ 2500 people.

After retiring seven years ago, Sulzberger returned as temporary chief executive in the Spring of 2023 to help transform Calida again. He could see that HR programmes designed to update the culture were having a limited impact. Instead, he concluded that people had to find the solutions themselves. 'It's much easier than if you try to dictate them.'

'We want to have a common culture and a common mindset. Then each brand can operate independently. So we communicate intensively with everyone. From head office, we are out all the time. We interact with everyone and are open in sharing information, good and bad.'

'Once a year we bring all our leaders together at one of our seven locations, doing a two-day workshop with culture and mindset as a key topic.'

'We then track what everyone in the company is thinking through polls. We're not interested in passive answers to multiple choice questions. We are looking for active responses and comments about what they are really feeling. We might be a public company now, but we want to remain family in spirit.'

Conclusion

As a leader, like Felix Sulzberger, you can find yourself putting employees at the centre of everything you do. As a process, you can adopt the principle of design thinking and customer experience to embrace all the moments that matter for your employees so you meet their expectations more fully and compete for the best talent. Or you can take an even wider, more transformational view about how to get your people on the bus, putting them at the centre of the new environment in which you are going to operate and compete after the pandemic.

Sources

- 'Rethinking your approach to the employee experience', Gartner, *Harvard Business Review*, March/April 2022
- 'This time it's personal: shaping the new possible through employee experience', Jonathan Emmett, Asmus Komm, Stefan Moritz, and Friederike Schultz, McKinsey & Co, September 2021
- *The Employee Experience Advantage: How to win the war for talent by giving employees the workspaces they want, the tools they need, and a culture they can celebrate*, Jacob Morgan, Wiley, March 2017
- Employee Experience Examples: 8 Companies that Offer Great EX in the Workplace', Mary Madhavi Reddy, Emplus, April 2022
- *So you want to be Customer Centric*, Alain Thys, Future Lab, 2011
- 'It's not about the office, it's about belonging', Aaron De Smet, Bonnie Dowling, Marino Mugayar-Baldocchi and Joe Spratt, McKinsey & Co, January 2022
- 'Help your employees find purpose – or watch them leave', Naina Dhingra, Andrew Samo, Bill Schaninger, and Matt Schrimper, McKinsey & Co, April 2021
- 'What Is the Purpose of Your Purpose? Your why may not be what you think it is', Jonathan Knowles, B. Tom Hunsaker, Hannah Grove and Alison James, *Harvard Business Review*, March/April 2022

Growth Employee experience **Diversity and inclusion** Innovation Partnerships Business People Inspiration LEADER'S DRIVERS Digitalization Customer focus Process Market Effectiveness Brands Strategy execution Personalization

9.

LEADERSHIP FOR DIVERSITY AND INCLUSION

It might seem unusual to adopt courage as a core value for a manufacturer normally associated with systems conformed for quality. Courage to speak up. Courage to disagree. Courage to have an opinion. Courage to say who you are.

It's an expansive expression of what is meant by diversity and inclusion. It goes well beyond good HR practice and legal observance, which just represent the starting point. What makes courage matter to this engineer is the impact it will have on the business as a whole.

In an unpredictable world, teams are now finding themselves tasked with responding to complex challenges that cut across disciplines and domains. According to MCE, if you assemble them from those with similar profiles, you will consistently produce the same number of solutions in the given time. That's fine if you're willing to accept middling performance.

The alternative is to put together a team with dissimilar backgrounds. However, left to themselves, they will find fewer solutions and take more time. Why? Because they have too many conflicts between them.

However, if before this team starts, each member explains why they're different, it will find more answers in less time. In other words, aside from the benefits of social responsibility, it makes business sense for a manufacturer to encourage a robust culture of diversity and inclusivity. Which of the three outcomes transpires in response to a challenge, middling, weak or strong, then depends on how leaders choose to translate principles such as courage into practice.

'Historically, diversity and inclusion has been about engaging people and avoiding lawsuits,' says Jann Jevons, a member of the MCE faculty. 'Organizations were mainly on the defensive.'

'Now leaders are starting to think it's crazy to let talent go to waste. Many studies are proving that a commitment to D&I is making an impact on how organizations perform,' says Jevons, who was on BT's fast-track programme for talented young women and who joined its HR strategy team.

'Even so, it's extraordinary when you see corporate values being changed to include a word like courage. In the world of D&I, it's massive, because it's a voice for those who don't feel they've been given a fair shot.'

Commitment and impact

A commitment to diversity and inclusion is now becoming widespread among organizations. By 2020, their total spending had reached $7.5 billion, which is expected to keep growing by 12.6 percent a year to reach $15.4 billion in 2026, according to a recent report by Global Industry Analysts.

In their view, it is becoming 'a global gold rush for multicultural markets, diverse employees and untapped consumer bases'. Inclusivity is giving companies the potential to 'spearhead growth by leveraging their access to a diverse talent pool', enhancing their potential for creativity and innovation. However, it also challenges long-held assumptions about how companies recruit and operate.

In a report in 2020, McKinsey confirmed that more diverse representation leads to better performance. For gender, the most diverse companies were 48 percent more profitable than the least. For ethnic minorities, the difference was 36 percent.

Yet, despite these figures, it found that progress remains relatively slow. Women on executive teams rose from 15 to 20 percent in the five years from 2014. Ethnic minorities were up from 7 to 13 percent.

Furthermore, numbers are unevenly spread across organizations, as a divide opens between high and low performers. A third of companies are making real improvements and gains. The rest have made or little no progress. Some are even going backwards. As a laggard, whether in the slow lane or on the side of the road, the penalty to your profitability is 27 percent.

So what is happening to everyone's good intentions and extra spending? It appears that commitments to D&I are relatively easy to make. They are proving much harder to implement. Among the workforces and talent pools of these laggards , according to McKinsey, disappointed expectations are overwhelmingly channelled one way: at their leaders.

Two priorities for leaders

Diversity is about recruiting a broader mix of people in the workplace. Inclusivity is about making them feel part of a culture and working together as a whole, based on respect for everyone's different backgrounds.

In response, leaders have two priorities: externally, what the law requires and what society expects; and, internally, what they themselves think and value, not just in how they communicate their organization's message, but how they see its future.

In most places, the law is specific about how you recruit for all posts, including the composition of your board. My first encounter with such anti-discrimination was in California in the 1990s, when attending an executive programme at the University of Berkeley. Under the rules, no account could be made for age, gender or origin at the risk of severe consequences. As director of a Belgian specialist in the immersive learning of languages, we were thankfully already used to working across different cultures.

Recruiters are now highly aware of the potential damage to an organization's reputation if anything goes wrong. As a leader, however, the question is not just how to defend yourself, it is about how to benefit from becoming more socially aware.

In the 2000s, I was MCE's vice president for business development in the Gulf. No one would question the traditionally male orientation of these markets. In Saudi, women could not drive or go alone to the supermarket.

Suddenly, the country's vision shifted towards more opportunity for women and greater diversification of the economy. Under its policy of womenization, you were finding women in senior positions. How were such dramatic changes in culture to be managed in the daily context of running a business? How were interactions now going to happen between women and men as colleagues?

At such moments, it is all about leadership. You can do the minimum to respect what the law now requires and what society expects. Or you can turn it to your advantage.

At MCE, we had a similar experience in Portugal in 2019 at an event about women as leaders. It's a country where their representation has lagged behind elsewhere in Europe. A law was just being introduced setting a minimum of 33 percent representation at board level.

At the event, largely attended by male directors from the boards of Portuguese corporations, the discussion soon turned to the new law: how will we find women who understand an engineering business like ours? how do we prepare leaders to collaborate? how will our financial performance improve?

At this point, it's time for leaders to broaden their thinking and ask themselves instead: what are the characteristics of leaders who believe that diversity can enhance their results? why do they build diverse teams? what can age, culture, background, origin, handicap and orientation bring to our company and to our teams?

The potential upside, as we have seen, is that together you can look at the picture from different ways and find creative solutions that you would not otherwise have envisaged. It will only happen by taking an equally fresh look at your communications, your processes, your alignment and your culture.

We are not talking about doing it all at once. You can start by making relatively small adjustments, which in time have unexpectedly transformative effects, as happened at the US pharmacy giant, Walgreens.

Breaking down invisible walls

It began with a resolution to find more opportunity in life for an autistic son. It ended with the US pharmacy chain, Walgreens, employing 2000 of those with disabilities in its 20 distribution centres across the country at the same level of performance and at the same level of pay as everyone else.

The results have been far better than anyone expected, including Randy Lewis, the logistics director, whose experience with his own son inspired him to give hope to the 44 percent of Americans with disabilities who can't find a job.

It started as a small experiment with the disabled working on merchandise and custodial. They rapidly proved themselves as equal to the task as anyone else. As a result, the first of a new generation of warehouses was built in South Carolina in 2007 with a target to employ a third disabled.

Performance levels were not just as high as anywhere else. They were the best in Walgreen's history. The experiment was then extended nationwide with the same target of a third disabled everywhere.

'We didn't have to be reminded that we're a business not a charity,' Lewis told a TEDx meeting in Naperville in 2015. 'We weren't going to lower the bar. If anything, we were going to raise it because these centres were designed to be the most advanced.'

'We studied thousands of hours across multiple centres across multiple jobs. People with disabilities perform as well or better. They work safer.'

Once he had straightened out any attitudes in the workforce between them and us, Lewis was surprised about the impact that the initiative had on the whole culture of the business. 'We had to learn to never assume what people can and cannot do.'

'People now talk about teamwork and commitment like they've never done before. Managers say they have had to become better listeners. They had to learn how to treat people as individuals.'

'They will now say my number one job now is to make everybody around me successful. When you have everybody aligned toward mission and everybody doing their job to make others successful, you've got lightning.'

For Lewis himself, it has all been about: 'people who want to work, who can work, but aren't allowed to, because of the invisible walls that we build around our businesses.'

Transformational models

The question is whether Walgreen's experience was just a happy combination of circumstances: a leader inspired by his son, an early mover advantage in reaching out to the disabled and a culture that responded to the initiative. In other circumstances, it could have fared less well. You can't just rely on finding such inspirational leaders all the time.

In pursuing a transformational model, the danger is that you commit to the goals without following through and lose the confidence of your workforce. So how have some of the best performers created a culture of D&I that everyone can consistently buy into?

There is nothing miraculous about it. They are just following the path from a requirement for diversity to a culture of inclusivity in the same way as Walgreen grew from a small initiative to recruit the disabled.

Other companies start, for instance, by holding gender workshops for women. When participants say it would help if everyone, women and men, were to attend, follow-up sessions can be held about building a culture around authenticity or courage.

Companies like Accenture, Mastercard, Abbot, Eli Lilley and BASF have then started to reach further to include equity and belonging within a more comprehensive model, such as DEIB which is now setting the pace, where:

- Diversity is about demographics (gender, origin, age, orientation).

- Equity is ensuring an equal chance to all candidates whatever their background.

- Inclusion is about fair treatment with respect, whatever the difference is.

- Belonging is about the feeling of being accepted in the workplace.

Without equity, diversity will remain an empty promise if access is not actively open to all. Everyone has to have a chance to progress, unlimited by where they might live or how they might travel. Where gaps or limitations exist, coaching or mentoring are put in place to build confidence.

Similarly, belonging is the result of creating an inclusive culture in which everyone feels genuinely able to bring all of themselves to work.

Metrics

If DEIB as a model is to become more than an aspiration, it has to be measured. However, as highlighted by Joan C Williams and Jamie Dolas in the *Harvard Business Review* (March/April 2022), it brings two particular sets of problems in collecting data, which can result in patchy analysis and faulty interventions.

First, company lawyers and line managers worry that if they collect data, they will create liabilities that could end up as lawsuits. However, it's not them who should be deciding what risks can be tolerated. It's up to senior leaders to create a policy based on DEIB as a business goal and to communicate it throughout the organization.

Second, data is mainly collected about outcomes, ie, how many women or ethnic groups are employed in what positions. These give a clear baseline for judging bias and measuring progress. However, they only indicate whether you have a problem. They don't tell how you to fix it.

So, add metrics to track the employee management process, say Williams and Dolas. If you are falling short of diversity targets, you will then know with more certainty whether the problem lies with hiring, evaluation, promotion or executive sponsorship.

More positively, if you establish a clear set of data about how you are performing against your DEIB goals, you can track progress against your peers, identifying the next gaps in your performance that you would like to address.

Implementing DEIB

You can't just launch a few initiatives and workshops for diversity and inclusion without risking a backlash from your talent pool. The challenge for leaders is to align their teams and operations at all levels, creating a real culture of diversity and inclusion.

In our work at MCE with organizations in navigating DEIB and making it a part of their DNA, here are the five steps we recommend:

- Incorporate it into your corporate culture and business strategy. Start from the top, create a common language and be clear about the benefits, so everyone understands.

- Develop standards of respect and acceptance. Share the vision throughout the organization. Highlight expected behaviours. Cascade them through workshops. Learn too how to identify harassment and disrespect.

- Get managers to understand and implement inclusive leadership so they can promote it every single day.

- Create a respectful workplace for everyone. Coach managers to foster positivity and inclusivity. Maintain consistency when it comes to respect.

- Overcome unconscious bias. Be aware of its negative impact. Learn strategies to overcome it.

1	Incorporate it into your corporate culture
2	Develop standards of respect and acceptance
3	Get managers to understand and implement
4	Create a respectful workplace
5	Overcome unconscious bias

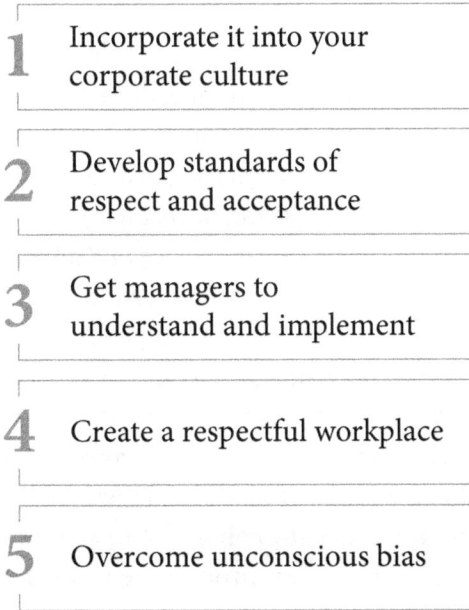

Figure 1: five recommended steps to make DEIB part of your company's DNA (source: MCE)

The Global Parity Alliance in its 2023 report, *Diversity, Equity and Inclusion*, launched at the World Economic Forum, added five further factors for success:

- Nuanced understanding of root causes.

- Meaningful definition of success.

- Accountable and invested business leaders.

- Solutions designed for context.

- Rigorous tracking and course correction.

Strategic lens

Unlike innovation, which is an unquestioned strategic priority in many organizations, DEIB is still establishing itself as a core goal among leaders, even if it is proving itself as a differentiator in attracting talent, generating ideas and making decisions.

For those high performers who do use it as a strategic lens to improve performance in their value chain of talent, suppliers and customers, it is letting them leverage all these assets to generate superior financial returns, as well as creating a more vibrantly modern business culture.

The extent to which these outcomes are achieved will depend on the choices that leaders make, says Jann Jevons at MCE. 'Many take the first step and run a series of modules. However, D&I is integral to building a culture. It starts with being able to attract the right people to the organization, it then goes through the whole lifecycle, not only of the employee, but also of every product that's designed and every service that's delivered.'

Illustration: diversity and inclusion at Kurita

Kurita is a leading force in treating water, creating solutions for purity and efficiency, as well as helping to design the module for its supply to the International Space Station. Originally from Japan, Kurita now has plants all over the world. In Europe it is a solution provider for industrial water treatment. In moving forward, the company's ambition is to co-create more value with its customers for the benefit of society, as well as taking a lead on net zero.

'We want to be as open as we can to working with people from different backgrounds and different cultures,' says Tanja Sanders, Kurita's director for human resources in Europe, the Middle East and Africa.

Three years ago, her division began a programme for gender diversity. It included a series of interviews with role models and some mentoring. 'We have opened it up to everyone now,' she says, 'because diversity is everyone: younger, older, women, different backgrounds.'

The programme is now expanding to include team training, as well as guidance on unconscious bias. 'It's not a one-off project for us. We want to live it. It's an awareness we are expecting from everyone. We are making it an integral part of our leadership development at all levels.'

'From our people's point of view, we want an environment where it is psychologically safe to speak. As a rationale for our business, it makes us more efficient and more innovative.'

The knowledge that Kurita has gained in Europe is now spreading through the rest of the group. A diversity and engagement section has been created in Japan with a set of nine actions to support the company's overall vision of creating shared value by working with people from all kinds of background.

Diversity reinforces everyone at Kurita's sense of purpose in responding to the challenge of net zero. Cuts in energy consumption and waste are integral to what it offers. It is also active in supporting sustainability projects and responding to natural disasters.

'For us, it's not a question of installing diversity. We want it to become a normal way of acting, thinking and behaving for everyone, ingrained in our DNA and part of our culture.'

Sources

- *Global Parity Alliance: Diversity, equity and inclusion lighthouses*, World Economic Forum in collaboration with McKinsey & Company, 2023
- *Five key steps to making D&I part of your company's DNA*, MCE: mce.eu/strategic_areas/diversity-inclusion/
- *Diversity Wins: How inclusion matters*, a report by McKinsey & Company, May 2020
- *Global Diversity and Inclusion Market*, a report by Global Industry Analysts, November 2021
- 'Data Driven Diversity', Joan C Williams and Jamie Dolas, *Harvard Business Review*, March-April 20222
- *What is Diversity, Equity, Inclusion and Belonging?*, Findem's knowledge centre: findem.ai/knowledge-center
- *Why I hired a workforce no one else would*, Randy Lewis, former vice president, Walgreens, TEDx Naperville, 2015, YouTube
- 'Women's Management in Portuguese Listed Companies', *Eco News*, 2019.

10.

LEADERSHIP FOR INSPIRATION

Inspiration is about creating a vision for the future and generating the belief to make it happen. In its pure form, it is how someone like Richard Branson, the founder of the Virgin Group, keeps establishing so many new businesses.

Few of us are such naturals. However, inspiration is not just about charisma. Force of personality only takes you so far. If your team can't translate your vision into reality, performance is sure to plateau.

We all know leaders too who shine in the limelight. However, if the image and the credibility of the venture is just about them, it can unravel in the exposure.

Instead, inspiration is about a set of behaviours. We can all learn to inspire in our own way. Both those at the top and those in the wider leadership team. For each of them, it's within their power to inspire people to take the extra step and achieve the improbable.

How do you recognise an organization driven by inspiration? Listen to everyone's pitches and speeches. They always refer to the leader. It's a sure sign. Some of these inspiring leaders are omnipresent, of course, but they are not always the only ones. The challenge is to cascade this inspiration so it drives performance everywhere.

Inspiring a shared vision

Perhaps one of the most famous and unexpected moments of inspiration came before the final of Rugby World Cup in 1995. In the film, Invictus, South Africa's first black president, Nelson Mandela, talks to Francois Pienaar, the captain of the Springboks, the country's team and once proud symbol of the apartheid regime.

Mandela never directly encourages Francois Pienaar to win the final. Instead, more powerfully, he says, we need inspiration to become a united country. 'Because in order to build our nation, we must all exceed our own expectations.'

Exemplary leaders, such as Mandela, envision the future, creating and sharing a unique image of what a team, an organization or a country could become, say Jim Kouzes and Barry Posner in *The Leadership Challenge*, a foundational study of effective leaders at their personal best in all walks of life.

'Through their magnetism and persuasion, leaders enlist others in their dreams. They breathe life into their visions and get people to see exciting possibilities for the future.'

Such leaders, they observe, 'have a tremendous impact on the motivational levels of others, as well as workplace productivity ... Leaders who express conviction and enthusiasm about the future, no matter their role or title, are consistently seen as more effective.

Leaders who wake up and hit the ground running towards their vision are leaders that people love to rally behind.'

For some, it comes naturally. For others, these are behaviours to learn, particularly if you are going to looking to adopt inspiration as a driver for your organization.

Leading with Virgin

Perhaps it's because he made his first fortune as a record producer in the early 1970s, but Richard Branson was among the first to realise the potential of leaders as conductors not soloists, as the power of hierarchical authority was being replaced by a style of inspirational leadership that people wanted to follow.

In *Business the Richard Branson Way*, Des Dearlove reports that one of Branson's great talents is: 'getting people fired up about a new business idea and then letting them loose on it. His own enthusiasm is contagious, focusing excitement on a goal or destination which then allows him to step back and let others run with it. Somehow, too, he spurs people on to achievements they wouldn't have believed possible'.

Branson and his team review numerous business proposals a week. Most are rejected, a few become a new Virgin company. 'It is one thing to recognise potential for a business and quite another to make it a reality. This is one of Branson's secrets: the ability to make it happen. He is the catalyst that triggers a chain reaction that transforms potential energy in a project or idea into kinetic energy that sends people scurrying people in a thousand directions.'

Becoming inspiring

Real breakthroughs in performance at Virgin and elsewhere come from employees who feel inspired by their leaders. In reality, many organizations are still falling well short.

In a survey by Bain Consulting (*Harvard Business Review*, April 2017), less than half of respondents agreed their leaders were inspiring. Even fewer felt their leaders encouraged engagement and represented the values of the organization.

So is all lost? Not according to Bain's author of the report, Eric Garton. He identifies 33 traits within four areas: developing inner resources, connecting with others, setting the tone and leading the team.

'We found that people who inspire are incredibly diverse – there is no universal archetype. A corollary of this finding is that anyone can become an inspirational leader by focusing on his or her strengths. Although we found that many different attributes help leaders inspire people, we also found that you need only one of them to double your chances of being an inspirational leader.'

However, inspired performance can be undermined by mediocre outcomes. 'Inspiring leaders use their unique combination of strengths to motivate individuals and teams to take on bold missions – and hold them accountable for results.'

Inspirational models

For the head of HR for Digital.ai in North America, Heidi Lynne Kurter there are seven characteristics that stand out among the relatively small handful of truly inspirational leaders. (*Forbes*, February 2020):

- They stay true to their values and don't cave under the pressure of situations where they might be compromised.

- They realize they are probably not the smartest in the room and are constantly looking for feedback to improve.

- They're the same person at work as at home and are open to sharing their own struggles and stories.

- They know the strengths and weaknesses of their team, encouraging a spirit of unity and collaboration.

- In conversations, they're good at picking up cues and can communicate negative feedback in a way that doesn't disengage someone.

- They're approachable and inclusive, creating a sense of belonging at work and making sure everyone is treated respectfully.

- They're ready to take courageous risks and learn from their mistakes.

'Their optimism and passion to achieve their vision demonstrates that there's always a solution,' says Kurter, 'even if it takes some setbacks and new plans.'

Cascading inspiration

A venture's switch from personality to culture is one of its classic points of transition as they grow. The question is how to move forward from the sense of creative freedom that a founder brings to a more devolved system for taking decisions and delivering value?

The tension between the two can become uncomfortable. At this point, the limits on future growth are often circumscribed by how leaders behave. It can be difficult to let go of the responsibility for the day-to-day reality of high-level performance and focus on the wider competitive challenges that will define how a venture now evolves.

It is a position in which Jean-Charles Samuelian-Werve has found himself twice. First, in revolutionising the design of aircraft seating. Now as the founder of Alan, launched as a one-stop health partner for employers, shaking up a previously a comfortable market, which had been slow to embrace digital and re-imagine customer service.

Since launching this vision in 2016, Alan now has 20,000 customers, a team of 500 and revenues of €280 million. Currently, it's operating in France, Belgium and Spain, but is now looking to expand by one country a year.

The reward for founders, such as Samuelian-Werve, who can sustain their vision while building a significant level of organizational complexity, is a significant rise in capital value. So how does leadership start to operate on such a scale and what does 'inspire' now mean?

As a first step, we say at MCE, step back and define the ways in which your leader is inspiring. What are those in reality? Which of them can be replicated with sense? Which can cascade down? In parallel, you will clarify:

- The experience you are trying to create for customers.

- The behaviours required to meet those expectations.

- The narrative that everyone can relate to support those behaviours.

- The passion and belief that everyone in the organization shares.

Then you will be in a better position to say what role your inspiring founder now plays. It is all about aligning the passion to inspire leadership at each stage of an organization and a story that can be shared by all.

Inspiration in three behaviours

For Ramesh Fatania, who now runs MCE's programme for senior leaders, inspiration comes down to three behaviours: talk, walk and walk the talk. His own career was forged at BP under the inspirational leadership of John Browne in the 2000s, who saw a greener future for oil and gas, re-positioning the company and growing it from number seven to number three in the world.

Today's talent is looking to be inspired by more than a two-year return on capital, he says. 'They respond to aspiration and intent. So leaders are expected to articulate the wider context in which you are all operating, setting out a roadmap you are going to follow.'

These conversations happen at all levels to give people a sense of meaning and support. With John Browne, he says, you always felt big things were possible and he was relying on you as one of BP's future leaders. 'He made you feel part of that ambition to be the best in the world, creating growth and doing things differently.'

Face to face is also part of inspiration. As leaders, you have to walk, not just sit in front of your laptop and make conference calls. 'If you really sit down with people, look each other in the eye and have a dialogue, rather than a monologue, they will grasp the intent better. For them the biggest question is how can I participate in the journey to take us there? It becomes much more meaningful face to face.'

When Fatania was running some terminals for a BP joint venture with Shell, the director of engineering came to see him for two days. 'We drove around talking about what investments we could make to improve. It was not just me who felt valued. It was the whole workforce. We might just have been a small subsidiary, but we mattered.'

Then you have to walk the talk, he says. 'Leadership is becoming more human-centric. People expect you to be open about yourself and be authentic. So you have to uphold the values and standards you are following. If you don't, then no one is going to be inspired and you'll lose their trust.'

Leadership presence

Inspiration often happens in the moment. The first encounter with someone can make all the difference. So on MCE's programme for senior leaders, Fatania always gives participants 24 hours' notice to give a three-minute speech about a change they would like to make. No aids. No prompts. No slides.

'It is too easy to hide behind a presentation. It's too clinical. What people want to see is simplicity and how deeply you feel about it. Are you being true to yourself? Are you being authentic? It's a great way of giving leaders a sense of their presence.'

'Charisma helps, of course, but it's being genuine that really persuades and convinces. People are quick to see through any distractions. They want to be inspired more by the content, the depth of your thinking and your trustworthiness. Then they will follow you towards what you are trying to create together.'

Illustration: an interview with Eric Domb, founder of Pairi Daiza

Eric Domb's vision to bring animals and humans together in authentically beautiful, spiritually uplifting surroundings is regularly recognised as Europe's best zoo. For him it's not just about caring for the physical heath of the animals, but their psychological wellbeing as well.

His view is that there are three categories of animal: domestic, wild and those raised in captivity. 'We care for the last of those with a wider view of supporting conservation in the wild.'

Over the last 30 years, he has built nine worlds around an old abbey in Belgium. Today, his zoo, Pairi Daiza, attracts two million visitors a year, employs 600 people, has revenues of €120 million, cares for 7500 animals and has won numerous international awards.

Each of his worlds faithfully recreates natural environments in which he seeks to bring animals and humans together with a shared sense of love. It is a legacy he wants to continue. Eight years ago, the company came off the Belgian Stock Exchange, when a billionaire put aside his normal financial instincts to buy the outstanding 30 percent of shares. Domb holds the remaining 70 percent. Together they intend that the pioneering work at Pairi Daiza in bringing animals and humans together will continue long into the future.

So how has all this inspiration come together? How did Domb find himself in the position of running Europe's most admired zoo? How can his vision be maintained amidst the realities of running what is becoming a large and complex operation? Now 62, how does Domb reflect on a path he never expected to take?

Originally a lawyer, it didn't live up to his sense of wanting to be useful to others. So he started advising smaller companies on realising their plans. Then by chance, he agreed to humour a colleague by accompanying her father-in-law to view an abbey that he was thinking of turning into a bird park. Domb was unconvinced, until he saw it.

Together they resolved to launch a business, although each had different versions of it. In any case, the father-in-law left in a few weeks. However, at the age of 32, Domb had found his purpose. Or, perhaps more accurately, his purpose had found him.

His first step was to write a perfect business plan. None of it worked, Domb is now happy to admit. Instead, he relied on an incredible sense of energy that came from finding his life's meaning: to share a love for beautiful nature with everybody.

'This gathering was a kind of spiritual survival for me. When we started with 20 people, it was hell. Those are the heroes of such stories as ours, not those working comfortably on strategy.'

In his view, it's a duty to make sure all those efforts become financially sustainable. 'I didn't build a limited company, because I loved it. It was not a goal; it was a condition. And I became a leader by necessity, that's the truth.'

He has relied on attracting talented people to help him transform his ideas into reality, Even now, he says, it remains his toughest, but most rewarding challenge. 'Conservation is not just a dream here. We have a real energy to do something. That's why we can attract such interesting people.'

Domb has a clear conception of his role: to make these dreams visible. 'If you don't push people to go beyond what they think they are capable of, they will not evolve as far as they could. They're able to do it all, even though they don't know it yet.'

Conclusion

So inspiration starts with leaders who have a clear vision and who passionately follow it through. It is something more than just ego. It often combines with other drivers: branding in the case of Richard Branson; digitalization and customer service for Jean-Charles Samuelian-Werve.

At Ryanair, the founder and chief executive, Michael o'Leary creates a buzz around operational excellence and pricing. His unswerving belief in this combination of drivers, which finds expression throughout the organization, is what has created one of Europe's most profitable airlines.

Sources

- 'Inspire a shared vision: How to create a common purpose', Jim Kouzes and Barry Posner, LeadershipChallenge.com, July 21
- *Business the Richard Branson Way: 10 secrets of the world's greatest brand builder*, Des Dearlove, Capstone, 1998
- 'How to be an inspiring leader', Eric Garton, Bain Consulting, *Harvard Business Review*, April 2017
- 'Seven powerful characteristics of a truly inspirational leader', Heidi Lynne Kurter, senior contributor, *Forbes*, February 2020

PART 4

MARKET

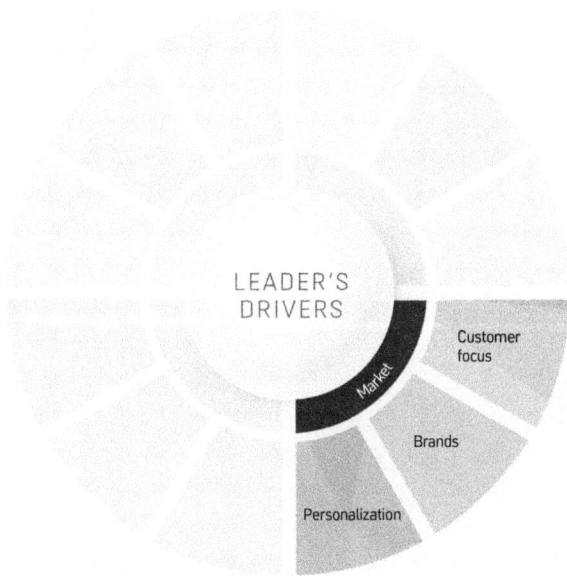

LEADER'S
DRIVERS

Customer
focus

Market

Brands

Personalization

The wheel diagram shows "LEADER'S DRIVERS" at the center, surrounded by segments including: Growth, Employee experience, Diversity and inclusion, Inspiration, Customer focus, Brands, Personalization, Strategy execution, Effectiveness, Digitalization, Partnerships, Innovation. Inner ring labels include: Strategy, People, Market, Process.

11.

LEADERSHIP FOR CUSTOMER FOCUS

Companies almost universally claim they are putting their customers first. It's easy to say, yet much harder to do. Too often, they take the internal view of what their customers would like or they make expensive improvements that no one really cares about. According to figures from Bain & Co and Satmetrix, 80 percent of chief executives believe their business delivers a superior experience, while only 8 percent of their customers agree. That tells you a lot.

It's not enough to check customer satisfaction once a year, when it is the minimum that they can expect from you. Instead, you would like to know in real time what it is that delights them about you and why they might recommend you to anyone else. Or, just as importantly, why they are disappointed and why they might make a complaint.

Customer surveys have their place, of course. However, most of the time they aren't telling you what really matters to your customers, particularly if they are being quickly asked five closed questions. Let's take a concrete example.

You call a bank and wait. Then you spend 15 or 20 minutes following umpteen options interspersed with annoying music, before getting somebody on the phone. Then you are asked in a survey how many times you called, how friendly the member of staff was and whether you got an answer to your question. What you would like to say instead is that the waiting time is totally unacceptable and frustrating, that you called three times but abandoned twice and that the menu is too long and annoying.

So it is no surprise that the results of such surveys are treated as soft signals compared to the hard financial numbers that everyone follows: targets for sales, budgets for project managers and returns for leaders. Those are what determine day-to-day behaviour.

However, it leaves you vulnerable to upstarts who more genuinely articulate what customers really value. So how can leaders bridge the gap? how can they put customers at the centre of their operations and their planning for the future? how can they give more weight to the views of those on the frontline? what behaviours do now they expect from everyone else in the organization? and how, ultimately, can they make sure they are making good profits, not bad profits?

Bad profits, good profits

Financial accounting, for all its sophistication and influence, ignores the main way we make an impact in business – and in life – through the people we touch, says Fred Reichheld in his book, *The Ultimate Question 2.0* (Harvard Business Review Press, 2011). Even if we can see that many of the winners in today's transparent markets are those who put customers first, the culture of most companies remains staunchly profit-centric, ruled by financial budgets and accounting metrics.

'While bad profits don't show up on the books, they are easy to recognise,' says Reichheld. 'They're profits earned at the expense of customer relationships. Whenever customers feel misled, mistreated, ignored or coerced, profits from that customer are bad. Bad profits are about extracting value from the customers, not creating value.'

It doesn't have to be this way, he says. Some companies have learned to tell the difference. 'Good profits are earned with customers' enthusiastic co-operation. A company earns good profits when it so delights its customers they willingly come back for more ... in effect, they become part of the company's marketing department, not only increasing their purchases, but also providing enthusiastic referrals'.

The paradox of growth

At the start, business is almost always personal. Just take a walk around any market. Everyone knows all their buyers and suppliers. 'Those who have fresh fish do best,' says Olivier Courtois on the MCE faculty and a leadership coach to numerous companies in the Middle East. 'Those who try to get rid of their rotten fish lose business. You're in close proximity to your customers. A passion for pleasing and helping the other side makes a difference.'

'The paradox is that to create more value, you have to scale up. That's where the problems start. Not everyone is facing the customer anymore. It's easy to forget them. Yes, you have to capture the advantages of size, but at the same time keep the agility you had when you were small.'

So give a voice to those on the frontline, he says. When he was managing retail and wholesale at Levi Strauss in the 2000s, it used to take 18 months for a new shape or colour of jeans to reach the shelf. Then Zara arrived as a competitor and took six weeks.

'If someone has an idea or insight, let them check it out. Create bubbles of risk. Give them three months to make it work. Then together you can assess where you are.'

You may well find yourself riding the next wave of what customers want. 'However, if it grows faster than you are developing your talent, the market will go to your competitors. That's particularly true if you are shifting from one model to another. You can buy in skills, but it's expensive. It's better to build your own talent.'

It's also a question of making sure you have the right systems in place to empower those serving customers, he says. At Etihad, the leading Middle East airline, the chief executive travels incognito on flights to make sure that every detail is right for passengers. It became clear that to attract more international flyers, the airline would have to start serving alcohol, despite the airline's Muslim origins. The view of all the cabin crews were respected about whether they were comfortable serving it or not. 'However, big you become,' says Courtois, 'don't become a heavy machine. Remain agile enough to keep customer service at the centre.'

A seamless experience

Digital is making all markets more transparent. However, the underlying structures and channels for distributions often come from an age where business had more control. It's hard to shake the assumption that customers are obedient subjects who will shop where and how we tell them, says Alain Thys on the MCE faculty and author of *So you want to be customer-centric?* (Futurelab, 2011).

'National organizations are still the norm. Marketing and sales are separate departments. Selective distribution contracts lock buyers and sellers into behaviours and business models that have gradually stopped making sense.'

'As a result, margins are wasted. Sales opportunities are lost. Customers switch to brands, retailers and vendors that offer them the transparency and multi-channel service they seek.'

'The only way to truly capture customer loyalty is to build a relationship that goes way beyond your product or your distribution set-up. The experience you offer across channels will in fact become your product.'

'You will need to keep in touch with customers at an individual level. You will need to map and connect to the influencers that affect their decisions. Every touchpoint must be ready to instantly recognise each customer and engage them in a way that builds loyalty, advocacy and trust.'

In automotive, for instance, the industry has traditionally looked at customers from a dealer's point of view, where it is purchase and after-sales that matter. However, for customers, as Lexus found in 2011, the experience is completely different, comprising a series of ten touchpoints. If you can fulfil the brand promise at each of those, you are redefining your relationship with customers and putting yourself at a distinct advantage.

It's the inconsistencies and oversights that let you down, says Olivier Courtois. 'It's not just about the end point, which is usually the sale. It's about the pain points too. What are the blockers? If you put all those on a scorecard, you can start to measure how close you are coming to meeting customers' expectations.'

The ultimate question

So is there a way to bring all these different elements together and combine them in a single easily understood metric that everyone in the company can follow on a regular basis? It was a question that Fred Reichheld was pursuing as a consultant at Bain & Co in the early 2000s. He found that customer surveys were covering numerous indicators in a closed system against a defined set of assumptions. The results were no doubt useful, but too diffuse for everyone to follow.

He didn't want a focus on customers' satisfaction to be a box ticked once a year. He was looking for a metric that could track delight in real time. Through a process of elimination, he settled on one openly sourced, easily understood question: 'On a zero-to-ten scale, how likely is that you would recommend us to a friend or colleague?'.

In MCE's interpretation of his model, you then end up with three types of customers:

- Brand ambassadors (9-10) who recommend you to others.

- Passives (7-8) who are satisfied but won't recommend you.

- Brand assassins (0-6) who are dissatisfied and will share their negative experience with others.

Reichheld's next step was create a metric that everyone could follow: the percentage of customers who are promoters less the percentage who are assassins. It gives you the net promoter score (NPS), a bottom-line figure that everyone can follow and use.

One follow-up question was added: 'what is the primary reason for your score?'. It was a prompt with which anyone can explore what's happening. Whether on the frontline in sales and marketing or in operations such as finance or IT, everyone could exercise responsibility for the customer experience. It transforms a function like finance, which might once have thought it didn't deal with the customer. Now it is becoming an integral part of the experience you are creating.

The priority is to address the objections of your brand assassins. Their complaints might once have reached a dozen people. Now they can be seen by hundreds or thousands online. When the right person follows up, often from functions like finance or IT, it often results in a quick win.

Once you start bringing round your detractors, the next step is to start exploring how to bring delight to those in the middle, the passives, discovering how to give them more than the satisfaction that they have a right to expect as standard.

Business metrics

Through the NPS, such customer attitudes can become part of management accounts. Now the net present value of each customer can be added to the usual figures about revenues and margins, bringing a new, more accurate dimension to forecasts and risk analysis.

Customers who are more or less likely to repurchase can be separated. Clearer decisions can then be taken about profit margins. Future, not past, behaviour will determine portfolio decisions. Any cuts to costs will only be made after understanding what matters to customers and what they could live without.

This ability to put a financial value on customer delight is a huge step forward, says an MCE paper, creating a breakthrough in board discussions. Customer delight can no longer be dismissed as an expense. 'You can now put a numerical value on how much it generates versus how much it costs. The results might surprise you.'

Sparks need no longer fly when financial and customer data cross into each other's territory. 'Suddenly it is possible to estimate a return on customer initiatives. It puts them on the same footing as any operational investment decision.'

'Since your customers have different touch points in your organizations – call centres, repair partners, direct sales and logistics – resources can be allocated to the weakest areas. If the financial return on making customers more likely to recommend is bigger than the cost of doing so, an investment is worth making.'

Numbers into behaviours

Data and structure take you so far. Remarkable customer experiences are always created by people who are able to adapt to unique situations. As a leader, it is up to you to give everyone the freedom to make those moments happen by creating a code of behaviour by which you are all going to live and by setting the example yourself.

Alain Thys has kept a note of eight commitments made by senior teams seeking to becoming more customer-centric:

- spend a day personally talking to customers;

- consider the customer's voice when taking decisions;

- include customer objectives in performance reviews, including your own as a leader;

- give people time and resources to engage with customers;

- review customer feedback with their teams each month;

- go online to seek out customer comments at least once a month;

- include customer lifetime value in all financial and investment decisions;

- make a formal, quarterly effort to seek new ways of focusing on customers.

As a leader, if you can make and keep such pledges, it will make a powerful start in creating a customer-centric culture. The principle then has to flow through the organization as a whole, says Thys. 'Make sure they are willing and able. Organize events where they can reflect on these behaviours. Give them the skills to switch. Then remove any roadblocks. If the organization gets in their way, they'll soon get frustrated.'

Illustration: leading for customer-centric
Comment by Elia Congiu, chief HR officer, MSC Cruises

'MSC has transformed itself from a cruise line in the Mediterranean to a global powerhouse, offering voyages to captivating destinations worldwide. This strategic growth positions us as a versatile player, catering to varied traveller preferences and driving the evolution of our industry.

'Connecting performance with our growth focus at MSC Cruises involves a strategic shift towards a customer-centric approach, encompassing both onboard and shoreside teams. This shift means we've redefined our key performance indicators to encompass not only financial results but also guest satisfaction metrics like NPS and guest feedback ratings.

'Additionally, our investment in training and development programmes extends to shoreside staff, empowering them with the skills necessary to enhance the guest experience. Our online learning and development offering includes topics such as customer service, communication and conflict resolution skills, all aimed at delivering outstanding cruise satisfaction.

'We've also cultivated a culture of continuous improvement that applies universally, where both onboard and shoreside teams actively seek opportunities to enhance the guest experience, driven by regular reviews and action plans based on guest feedback. Leaders, whether onboard or shoreside, play a vital role in modelling this customer-centric approach, demonstrating its importance in decision-making and team interactions across the entire organization.

'In the face of a cruise market that's becoming increasingly appealing to customers, MSC Cruises has adopted a strategic approach that revolves around shifting from simply offering cruises to delivering a customer-centric experience. Our mission embodying our promise is to curate every aspect of our guests' holiday experience to provide lasting, meaningful memories.

'We prioritise guest satisfaction, use feedback for improvement, offer unique onboard experiences, and maintain a balance between customer happiness, profitability, and employee engagement. A satisfied workforce enhances the customer experience, leading to profitability.

'In addition, we've focused on digital transformation to provide modern travellers with a seamless and personalized journey from booking processes to onboard services. This strategic approach allows MSC Cruises to thrive in a market that's increasingly attractive to customers, offering them exceptional experiences that keep them returning.'

Conclusion

Leadership for customer focus is often less easy than expected. You can't rely on closed questions asked once a year in a survey. Instead, you want to know how your customers are feeling in real time. What are their expectations? what is happening at the touchpoints that matter most to them? Once you know, you can design your business around these experiences and create a culture where everyone's behaviour contributes to the delight that customers feel when dealing with you. For that to happen, it is up to leaders to find a way to empower people in front of customers.

Sources

- *The Ultimate Question 2.0: How net promoter companies thrive in a customer-driven world*, Fred Reichheld with Rob Markey, Harvard Business Review Press, September 2011
- *So you want to be customer-centric? A pragmatic guide to customer experience management*, Alain Thys, FutureLab, September 2011
- 'Is your CEO telling you to be customer-centric or customer-focused?', MCE paper, 2011

12.

LEADERSHIP FOR BRANDS

Brands lie at the point where strategy intersects with marketing, where logic meets emotion. For those who can clearly express who we are, what we do and why we are doing it, the rewards are rich: a premium on their sales and the most reliable way to future proof a business.

Much can and does go wrong. Interpretations vary about implementing it. User expectations change. Clarity erodes under pressure of making short-term returns. Too much faith is invested in breakthroughs.

Brands that once seemed dominant, such as Nokia, not only lose their shine, but can disappear altogether, victims of the end of one cycle and the start of another. By contrast, a brand like Virgin, whose original business selling records long ago disappeared, endures because its brand vision transfers to a new business.

As a leader, you are crafting a strategy for long-term survival, says Elina Panizza, a former brand strategist with Benetton and Motorola, who transformed the branding and image of two companies that I managed, aligning them to a premium strategy. 'Revolutions in business and society are now happening faster and faster. We can't even imagine how quickly the landscape will keep changing.'

'So your branding has to ingrain your vision at the heart of the company and deliver it to your publics. That's how you can future proof your company.'

Classic brands caught in the middle

Brand strategy is still often expressed as a pyramid: a few at the exclusive top, many at the bottom who buy what they can afford and those in the middle who aspire to more. In their heyday, brands appealed to everyone, finding a sweet spot in the middle where price, profit and volume coincided.

Those can be treacherous assumptions to hold, says a former president of the Levi's brand and president of Dockers, James Capon, who is on the MCE faculty. In a 2005 paper, he was already arguing that the middle is now 'a bite zone' polarised between brands that offer status and aspiration or convenience and efficiency.

Famously, Levi Strauss managed to escape this bite zone when it found itself drifting after its glory years during flower power and punk. Its marketing efforts were spread thinly across all its jeans, shirts and jackets, promoting one after another. Instead, in a brief originally written by Capon, it focused all its efforts into its most iconic pair of heritage jeans, the 501s, creating an ad where a young man takes them off in a launderette to a song by Marvin Gaye. It transformed the company.

Capon next found himself in the United States managing Dockers, a division of Levi Strauss that specialises in casual pants. After a promising start, it too was now in danger of falling into the bite zone, challenged by discounters at the bottom and aspirational upstarts at the top.

So Capon took the brand back to its core, focusing on its heritage as a supplier of khaki. Again, budgets were taken away from all the different product lines and put into one campaign. 'Internally, you're not going to make yourself popular', Capon admits, 'but after sales had fallen to $700 million, we got them up to $1.3 billion.'

New brands, value discipline and becoming number one

Capon's experience of escaping bite zones at Levi Strauss was part of a wider redefinition of the value that brands could offer and how they could compete. In the *Harvard Business Review* (January/February 1993), Michael Treacy and Fred Wiersema asked how newcomers, such as Nike and Dell, could establish themselves as industry leaders so quickly. How were they able to redefine value and raise customers' expectations beyond their competitors' reach? What is the influence that recognition, status and style now have in the choice of a brand?

'The idea that companies succeed by selling value is not new,' say Treacy and Wiersema. 'What is new is how customers define value in many markets. In the past, customers judged the value of a product or service as a combination of quality and price.'

'Today's customers, by contrast, have an expanded concept of value that includes convenience of purchase, after-sale service, dependability and so on. One might assume, then, that to compete today, companies would have to meet all these different customer expectations. This, however, is not the case.'

'Companies that have taken leadership positions in their industries in the last decade typically have done so by narrowing their business focus, not broadening it. They have focused on delivering superior customer value in line with one of three value disciplines: operational excellence, customer intimacy or product leadership. They have become champions in one of these disciplines while meeting industry standards in the other two.'

PRODUCT LEADERSHIP

Minimum
threshold
to compete

OPERATIONAL EXCELLENCE   CUSTOMER INTIMACY

Figure 1: the three value disciplines (Treacy and Wiersema)

'Companies that push the boundaries of one value discipline while meeting industry standards in the other two gain such a lead that competitors find it hard to catch up. This is largely because the

143

leaders have aligned their entire operating model to serve one value discipline.'

Brand definition

So how can leaders go about defining their brands and making them come alive? For Elena Panizza, a brand is best understood as the soul of a company. 'It's what gives meaning in the long term and sits at the heart of the business model.'

'It's a truth that resides within everyone at the company, not just leaders, but across all touchpoints. What is it that you do exceptionally well and makes you different? It's not always what you believe. The brand lives outside you, so you have to create a strong connection with those perceptions.'

Vision v mission

'When you have a clear vision,' says Panizza, 'you have the potential to adapt. You are not just seizing a temporary advantage. That's just being mission driven, which gives you value in the market today. But you can lose perspective of the bigger picture. Instead, as each transformation happens, brand leaders will translate their vision into the next set of missions.'

'That is how Disney has survived so many revolutions in the market. It is still about making people happy across all its different formats in entertainment and news. Virgin too has kept its original meaning for people, even though all its original record stores closed long ago. They are able to keep adjusting their mission to follow their vision.'

Symphonic v linear

Such meaning tends to be symphonic, says Panizza. 'After searching for your soul, you have to convert it into something more analytical. Business is numbers driven. You create a brand language and structure, like the brand pyramid, so everyone can understand it and apply it to different missions. This is our tone of voice and this is our interface. It gives you the tools to communicate.'

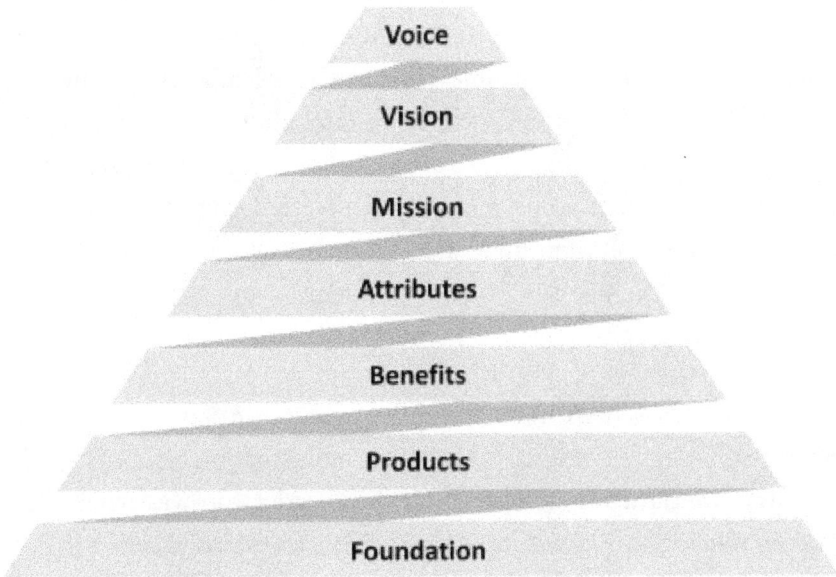

Figure 2: brand pyramid for leaders to cascade value into behaviours and actions

Brand implementation

For Levi Strauss, the core of the brand is product leadership: jeans so strong that the two horses on the patch on the back of every pair can't pull them apart. Such a powerful heritage can make it difficult to align everyone behind changes in the brand strategy.

Team alignment

As an Englishman shaking up marketing budgets in San Francisco, James Capon felt he was getting a lukewarm response to the repositioning of Dockers around its heritage in khaki, even though it was starting to show results. 'That's where leadership comes in,' he says. 'You have to drop down the organization and take a slightly messianic approach. We ran a series of workshops where we talked about what we were doing and why we were doing it, encouraging everyone to develop their own ideas.'

Trade-offs

Ideas were assessed within a triangle of value, similar to Treacy and Wiersema's. In operational excellence and customer intimacy, the industry standard was followed. Product leadership was where Levi Strauss was looking to set itself apart. 'This framework began to give everyone a sense of what trade-offs we could make in developing ideas.'

For instance, while some brands could offer customers sweatshirts in whatever colour they chose, Levi Strauss stuck to its catalogue, as it wasn't looking to exceed customer expectations. Instead, it chose to focus on fashions such as the distressed jeans worn by Bruce Springsteen. 'How could we make something of real quality, which you could wash a hundred times without falling to pieces? Even though everyone wanted to buy a pair, it was extraordinarily difficult to get our people to think like that.'

Living the brand

As a leader, for Capon, you should lead the lifestyle of your brand and be ready to show it to the world. While he was at Levi's, it was the start of smart casual at work, so it made sense to argue the case for the senior team to take off their suits and wear Dockers for a couple of days a week.

Capon then put on fashion shows in the head office and all the distribution centres. 'It was about what you could and couldn't wear. We assumed rightly that it would spread much more widely through word of mouth. I've always focused on trying to walk the talk and to live the kind of brand you want to be.'

The triangle of value

In 2001, Capon was in the running to become chief executive at Levi Strauss, but lost out to someone who wanted to focus more on selling jeans through retail, rather than competing on the brand's meaning. Since then, he has practised widely as a brand consultant.

'Where brands continue to go wrong,' he says, 'is when they try to please everyone and end up pleasing no one. Too many are not spending enough time on what the minimum has to be in their market and what really sets them apart.'

It's no easy task to reach the industry standard, he says. Take Ryanair, the low-cost airline, which competes on operational excellence and does the minimum really well. 'They're safe. They're on time. They're inexpensive. Everyone in the company knows what they're doing. Passengers know what to expect. That's why they are such a powerful brand.'

Illustration: tradition and renewal at Porsche

Dipl. Finanzing Mariella Ponearu, senior buyer at Porsche AG, comments in her own capacity on how, as a brand, Porsche is 'a company not just making cars but making dreams come true'

In 2018, the chair of the Porsche board, Oliver Blume commented on how digitalization, connectivity and electromobility will change Porsche's future strategy and brand identity. In a sentence, he was asked to summarise the brand identity: 'Porsche stands for exclusive sports car'.

'Our tradition is something we live out daily', he continued, 'but we also combine it with the future in order to develop further and create new things ... the great challenge remains being able to update brand values that have been formed by certain technologies once new technologies come along.'

'Identity, to me, is the answer to three questions. Who have I been? Who am I? Who do I want to be? Or, as applied to Porsche: Why do we exist? Why do customers buy our cars? What fascination do our cars hold? What drives us forward? What do we want to achieve? Once that is all clear and consistent, we will be perceived as differentiated, unique. Only then will we find inspired customers and responsible, passionate and motivated employees.'

'You have to let your identity continue to evolve. We are experiencing that at the moment. We are currently in the middle of a massive technological upheaval. Our model range has never been so varied; we have never before experienced such a cultural break in our thinking. It is important not to lose sight of the core. That is how I understand it.'

'Brand identity means that I recognise that it's a Porsche. Product identity means that I recognise which Porsche it is. We refer to this as a hierarchy of values.'

'I doubt that there is another car that has so frequently and consistently been adapted to match the requirements of a modern sports car and yet remained so unmistakeably true to its inner and outer values as the 911. In principle, the Porsche 911 is always the same sports car despite our uncompromising commitment to progress. Our company works in exactly the same way.'

'The essence of our brand, which can be found in every Porsche, regardless of whether it has two doors or four, regardless of whether it has an electric drive or not, regardless of whether it is purist or luxurious. This principle has made Porsche what it is and what it will continue to be.'

'Evolution instead of revolution. Always one step ahead. That is how we have always done it. Renew everything while retaining an irreplaceable identity.'

Conclusion

Leadership for branding is then clear. Leaders choosing to focus on brand must first define what the brand represents and what kind of behaviours it requires, consulting closely with their teams. Too often the concepts are far from the reality of employees and as a consequence they don't see clearly how to align their behaviour with the brand. Worse, they could misinterpret what is expected. So leadership for branding is a long exercise in defining concepts, translating them into behaviours, sharing them throughout the company and keeping everyone's focus on the brand and its attributes.

Sources

- The bite zone and how to escape it, a paper by James Capon, 2005
- 'Customer intimacy and other value disciplines', James Treacy and Michael Wiersema, *Harvard Business Review,* January-February 1993
- 'Digitalization, connectivity, electromobility. What will the future bring?', interview with the chair of the Porsche executive board, Oliver Blume, Porsche Newsroom, 2018

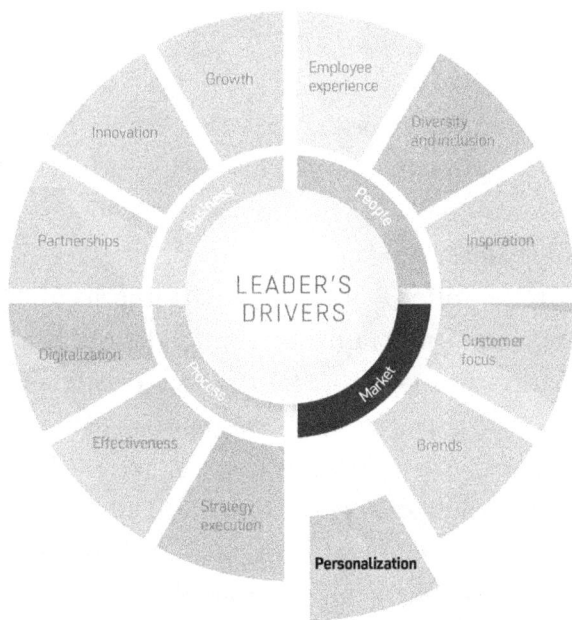

13.

LEADERSHIP FOR PERSONALIZATION

The age of the mass consumer is passing. Personalized products and services might once have been a premium extra. Now they are expected as standard. When data about everyone is so widely held, recommendations and offers can be made for each of us individually in real time: what might you like to watch? where would you like to go? is your health on track?

Such personalization applies at each point of a customer's experience with you. Get it right and you can earn 40 percent more (McKinsey) or your calls to action will have a 200 percent better rate of conversion (Hubspot), according to statistics collated by *Forbes* (February 2020).

However, such loyalty is fragile. Let personalization slip at any touchpoint and frustration soon mounts, as with 71 percent of shoppers (Segment) and 74 percent of web users (Instapage). If you're a transactional business, that may be fine. If you rely on building more lasting relationships with your customers, it's counterproductive to win them, only to lose them again.

It's why personalization is becoming such a priority for leaders, even if the advantage may predominantly seem to lie with digital brands. However, any organization has the scope to create experiences that meet the personal expectations and requirements of their customers.

'It's a battleground for customers', says Christian Dekoninck on the MCE faculty, who pioneered personalized customer service as a banker when setting up Citibank's first branch on the Champs Elysee. 'Customers are now so well informed and so demanding that the only way you can make a difference is through personalization. You have to make them feel special.'

'It's always a combination of the rational and the emotional. It is less about selling, more about what's best for your customers. It's where many companies find themselves going wrong.'

Customer intimacy

The classic definition of customer value as a combination of price and quality for the mass market started to fall apart in the 1990s, as customer intimacy established itself as one of three successors in competitive strategy. The other two, as Michael Treacy and Fred Wiersema argue in *The Discipline of Market Leaders* (Persueus, 1995), are price efficiency and product leadership.

They challenged the assumption that to become number one you start by identifying your core competencies. Instead, you first decide where to stake your claim in the market, then see what competencies and processes you require.

For those pursuing customer intimacy, it is not about the lowest price or the latest product features, but about the best total solution. Deep customer knowledge and breakthrough insights become your backbone. You're not trading at the leading edge, but tailoring your solution to fit each customer like a glove.

It's not just a question of how you present yourself or make sales. It takes the efforts of the whole organization. Together, you create a laboratory for developing better support, improving processes and intensifying the relationship. Innovation becomes a steady, controlled, incremental evolution.

You are looking for customers with relationship potential. It's not about one-off transactions or short-term revenue. You're happy to lay the foundation to make a larger, eventual return on investment.

To keep ahead, say Treacy and Wiersema, you will constantly search for new areas of untapped potential. That way, as a solution becomes standard and margins shrink, your knowledge of the customer will let you keep finding new ways to trade at a premium.

Personalization as standard

Such personalization might once have been a niche you could pursue at your own pace. Now it has become a widely held expectation. From their experiences online, customers see personalization as the default standard for engagement, says a 2021 report from McKinsey: it's what 71 percent expect when interacting with brands and 76 percent become frustrated when it doesn't happen. During the pandemic, it led to 75 percent of consumers to switch their buying and experiment with alternatives. Unless you give them an experience that makes them feel special, they'll go elsewhere.

Conversely, they respond positively when brands demonstrate their commitment to the relationship, not just the transaction, says

McKinsey. They like you to meet them where they are. Know their tastes. Offer something just for them. Check in. Preferences include:

- Ease of navigation (75 percent)

- Recommendations (67 percent)

- Tailored messages (66 percent)

- Targeted promotions (65 percent)

- Communicate at key moments (59 percent)

- Follow up after purchase (58 percent)

- Onboard after first purchase (51 percent)

For 76 percent, such personalized communications make them more likely to consider a brand. Even more, 78 percent, are more likely to repeat their purchase or recommend a friend.

Depending on how close you are to your customers, you can expect your revenues to grow by between 5 and 25 percent, if you get it right, says McKinsey: 'The more skilful a company becomes in applying data to grow customer knowledge and intimacy, the greater the returns.'

'Those leading the charge in personalization have better customer outcomes. Their focus on the relationship and long-term value leads to better upward migration, retention and loyalty.'

Intelligent customer engines

Personalization is now moving well beyond customer service. It is becoming central to how organizations compete, say David C Edelman and Mark Abraham in the *Harvard Business Review* (March-April 2022). At the cutting edge, 'intelligent customer engines' are being built that 'deliver personalization at a scale that could only have been imagined a decade ago ... we are now at the point where competitive advantage will derive from the ability to capture, analyse and utilise personalized customer data at scale and from the use of AI to understand, shape, customise and optimise the customer journey.'

The big tech companies are already well ahead, embedding personalization deeply into their business models. Brands, such as Starbucks and Nike, are following. Challenger brands are competing by designing transformative experiences with first-party data.

For those looking to catch up, it represents a time consuming, expensive and complex task. Even so, a merger between their customers' physical and digital experience may be the only way they can hold their own.

The best approach, say Edelman and Abraham, is to 'develop a data and tech road map with granular requirements tied to specific customer-driven use cases. Then bring together the business and tech teams to work iteratively, focusing on delivering the value as they build the foundation.'

They cite the example of Brinks, famous for its armoured vehicles, which increased its revenues by 9 percent by optimising its customer touchpoints across all channels, using AI to test thousands of messages and offers.

Such transformations follow the 70/20/10 rule: 70 percent people, 20 percent data and 10 percent the technology foundation. Even so, the results are likely to be experiences that are inconsistent, even stagnant, across channels, say Edelman and Abraham, unless five pivotal practices are followed:

- connect data signals and insights from an expanding range of sources;

- reimagine the end-to-end experience as a seamless flow powered by automated decisions;

- activate the experience across channels by connecting touchpoints;

- respond to the context of whoever and wherever customers are;

- experiment and test relentlessly.

'It's not just an exercise in journey mapping or technology planning. It is about developing the front-end flow to the customer and the back-end fuel to drive intelligent experience engines.'

Managing personalization

A commitment to creating a total solution for each customer has consequences for not just how you compete, but how you organize yourself and lead, an MCE paper was already saying in 2010. You will make yourself ready to partner with customers and assemble a team to solve their problems, often bringing in expertise from your supply chain. In structure, you will adopt a high degree of flexibility organizing yourself round the front end of what the customer requires, rather than being bound by product lines or brands.

You will aim to understand each customer as well as they do themselves and to learn from each solution you create. So, in style, your leaders will be entrepreneurial and knowledgeable. Then you will measure you progress by the profitability and loyalty of each customer, putting a high value on their lifetime value and guarding against the risk of their loss.

'If you want to be personalized, you have to empower people at the front end to find solutions for your customers', says Christian Dekoninck at MCE. 'It's no good relying on procedures. You have to find a solution for the customer immediately.'

'In inside-out organizations, where profits and costs come first, you can hurt your relationship with the customer. It takes leadership to become outside-in and say we are going to build win-win partnerships that will become much more profitable in the longer term.'

For Dekoninck, it raises two further questions: how psychologically can you relate better to each of your customers? and how can you best design solutions for them?

Personalized styles

To make the most of your customer relationships, it helps if you can flex to their preferred style. Based on the Insights method and Jungian psychology, Dekoninck draws three initial distinctions:

- Are you an introvert or an extrovert in your responses? do you reflect or speak out? are you observant or energetic?

- Do you think or feel when making decisions? are you objective or subjective? are you detached or considerate?

- Do you rely on sensation or intuition when absorbing information? is it the here and now that matters or imaginative potential?

These differences translate into eight types:

- Reformer

- Director

- Motivator

- Inspirer

- Helper

- Supporter

- Co-ordinator

- Observer

157

Once you recognise your customer's type (and your own), you can flex your style to communicate more effectively. In particular, if you are opposites, you can better manage the misunderstandings and conflicts that tend to occur not about what is said but how it is said. Once you can personalize your communications, barriers will fall and results will improve.

Designing the experience

For more human solutions, design thinking is a widely used technique for identifying what gains you can make for your customer and what pain you can relieve. You can create a more genuine and personal fit by being more open and empathetic.

First, you observe what you already know about your customer, then listen to what they are thinking and how they are feeling. Often it is best to have an open discussion, so they can give their side of the story, however unexpected it might be.

Now you will start to see gaps and what more you could offer. Only then do you start looking for solutions, drawing on ideas as widely as you can, often from different industries. Next you can build a pilot to test and adjust. You then either repeat the cycle or go live. Ultimately, you will find a combination of what is desirable for your customer with what is technically feasible and commercially viable for you.

Data analytics

Data is transforming the scope for creating more personalized solutions in real time. Historically, it was only gathered at the point of sale and expressed by customers themselves. Now online tracking is giving more context to preferences and behaviours, says a recent report by Deloitte about hyperperonalizing the customer experience.

Data collected internally can distinguish which customers drive the most value. External data, such as social media or credit histories, can fill in any behavioural gaps. With artificial intelligence, you can sift it all in real time and make decisions on the types of interactions to have with customers, whether it's an offer, a recommendation, an application or a message on a chatbot.

Personalization is not a single technology that can be installed, says Deloitte, but can be applied in a variety of ways through the customer journey. What you deploy depends on the impact you want to make. If it is customer loyalty, then connected communications are likely to be your priority. If it is quicker conversions, then the emphasis will be on personalized offers. That focus will give you the ability to leverage customer data at the most granular level.

Winning with AI

It's not inevitable that all the rewards for personalization powered by AI will go to big tech. Far from it. To realise the potential, it's time for leaders step up. In a recent article in the *Harvard Business Review* (March/April 2023), Thomas H Davenport and Nittin Mittal argue: 'AI – applied strategically and in large doses – will be critical to the success of almost every business in the future.'

'Data is increasing at a rapid pace and that's not going to change. AI is a means of making sense of data at scale and of ensuring smart decisions throughout an organization. That's not going to change either. AI is here to stay. Companies that apply it vigorously will dominate their industries over the next several decades.'

So far, in their view, AI initiatives at many organizations are too small and too tentative. 'They never get to the only step that can add economic value – being deployed on a large scale. Testing the waters may deliver valuable insights, but it probably won't be enough to achieve true transformation. A pilot programme or experiment can take you only so far.'

For leaders, the greatest challenge is creating a culture that emphasises data-driven decisions and actions and that makes employees enthusiastic about AI's potential to improve the business. 'In the absence of that kind of culture, even if a few AI advocates are scattered around the organization, they won't get the resources they need to build great applications, and they won't be able to hire great people. And if AI applications are built, the business won't make effective use of them.'

A single, inspirational leader will help, but without followers, AI initiatives will lapse. 'Ultimately commitment must go deep into the organization. If upper, middle, and even frontline managers are only paying lip service to the idea of transforming with AI, things will move slowly, and the organization will most likely revert to old habits.'

Illustration: personalization at Imerys

A commitment to customers is one of the competencies that Imerys expects from all its managers. As an industrial minerals company, it creates value-added solutions for a wide range of industries from automotive to consumer goods and healthcare. Based in France, it operates in 40 countries and employs 14,000 people. Sales are €4 billion in more than 130 countries.

Sales and technical application teams combine to gain a deep understanding of what their customers require and to speak the same language as they do. 'Being customer-centric is number one priority hand in hand with safety in our operations and sustainability', says Marianna Demiri, group talent director at Imerys. 'We want to be proactive in building long-term mutually beneficial relationships.'

Over the last three years, Imerys has run a programme of commercial excellence for the sales team, building their skills in negotiating and in finding value propositions. Individually, they have also worked with personal coaches to build their confidence in identifying areas for improvement in different industries and developing strategies to put forward. 'It's about having an open mindset and thinking creatively,' says Demiri. 'It puts us in a strong position, even in challenging financial and business environments.'

In early 2024, the talent team launched an updated framework of the competencies that makes a great leader at the company, following the purpose, vision and values defined for the group. The five leadership competencies they identified are based on an independent review of industry standards and input from senior leaders on the executive committee and HR team.

Commit to customers emerged as a clear imperative. The other four: were shape the future, care for self and others, collaborate for success and drive results.

'We want every single manager in the company to understand that what we do today has an impact tomorrow on us, on our planet and on our customers,' says Demiri. 'Our new leadership framework gives us a holistic view and we are expecting each manager to contribute to our strategy: it's not just top down, but bottom up and customer driven.'

Conclusion

Personalization is becoming central to how more and more companies now compete. For customers, the perception that matters is that you are treating them uniquely. Data and AI are transforming how you can communicate with them, what you can offer and what you decide. However, it is not enough. It takes leadership to make an organization truly outside-in, aligning your processes and rewards, so you can centre everything around responding to the personal preferences of each customer or, at least, giving them the feeling or perception, that is the case.

Sources

- '50 stats showing the power of personalization', Blake Morgan, senior contributor, *Forbes*, February 2020
- *The Discipline of Market Leaders*, Michael Treacy and Fred Wiersema, Perseus Books, 1995
- 'Customer Experience in the Age of AI: the case for building intelligent experience engines', David C Edelman and Mark Abraham, *Harvard Business Review*, March/April 2022
- 'The Age of Personalization: Crafting a finer edge', a report by Mastercard, *Harvard Business Review*, 2018
- 'The value of getting personalization right – or wrong – is multiplying', Nidhi Arora, Daniel Ensslen, Lars Fiedler, Wei Wei Liu, Kelsey Robinson, Eli Stein and Gustavo Schüler, McKinsey & Co, November 2021
- *Connecting Meaning with Experience: Hyper-personalizing the customer experience using data, analytics and AI*, Omnia AI, Deloitte
- *Are you having difficulties in the implementation of strategy and change? It could all be about leadership*, a report by MCE, 2010
- 'All-in on AI: How smart companies win big with artificial intelligence', Thomas H Davenport and Nitin Mittal, H*arvard Business Review Press*, March–April 2023

14.

LEADERSHIP WITHOUT AUTHORITY

This book has been about creating a distinctive sense of purpose and identity within your organization. It assumes you're operating with clear lines of authority. However, in reality, the workplace is becoming more ambiguous. Organizations now operate less as defined hierarchies and more as a series of flexible projects.

As a leader, you can find yourself responsible for an outcome, but have limited authority over those contributing to it. You might not have a title. It might not be recognised anyway. You might have no boss. Or you might have two with different agendas.

When authority is no longer automatic, resistance can build to the direction that a project is taking. Quality starts to vary. Deadlines slip. Differences turn into conflicts. So how do you get it all back on track?

It's a common scenario. You have acquired all the hard skills required to take a lead and you have the experience proving your professional worth. Now you are expected to exercise a range of soft skills to gain the support of unwilling colleagues, whose assumptions, cultures and timezones are different from yours.

You can make an appeal to authority, but you are only likely to win grudging acceptance from your team. Instead, it is better to rely on your own influencing skills, thinking more like a politician in assembling a coalition of interests. Even if you are in a weak or difficult position, you can bring together those with different agendas and different priorities.

It's not straightforward. We all have our own dominant style of influencing. Some of your colleagues will respond to you naturally. Others will take against you. It's exactly this sense of us and them that you want to deter.

So how can you use your influence to bring them together? First, realise your own influencing style is one among several, says Rajeev Aggarwal, a senior associate at MCE, who was global training director at Golden Tulip Hotels and sales operations manager at Fritolays International, a division of PepsiCo. Then adapt your style to suit different personalities and different circumstances.

Your colleagues on a project might not be assertive enough. They might talk more than they listen or more than they ask questions. They might rely too much on logic, too little on emotion. They might lack support to make their case. They might not have enough credibility. They may be too aggressive or accommodating in their defence. They might be striking the wrong note in how they communicate.

Such behaviours matter in flat organizations, such as the one where we were recruiting someone with a view to them becoming team leader. First, we said, adopt the influencing skills to inspire trust and gain authority. No, it turned out our recruit wanted the title first, then they would think about collaborating. Unfortunately, it doesn't work like that anymore.

Structures can cause tension too. In another organization, we were managing a network in ten countries. We controlled the overall budget and ran the marketing. Each of our country partners put in their own money and managed operations on the ground. If sales didn't turn out as expected, it would spark conflict after conflict. Who exactly was responsible for keeping the business going? When feelings run high, it is up to leaders to prevent such frustrations becoming destructive and maintaining a team of willing partners. So what steps can you take?

Create your power base

As an up-and-coming leader, you will be building your reputation for expertise and competence, which will give you a natural degree of authority. However, going forward, your influence will depend more on the quality of your network.

Partly it's about making business connections. It's also about allowing yourself to be human and finding emotional overlaps with others.

You might not necessarily like each other, particularly when you are building a coalition. So explore their interests and learn about their power base. Find out what really worries them. It might be their status or their career prospects. Then follow the reciprocal principle by giving something first, however small it might seem.

To make the right gesture, you will listen not just to what they are saying, but how they are saying it. They're unlikely to tell you what their interest is directly. So ask subtly smart questions too. 'What are the two or three main challenges in this situation?', for instance. Then rely on your intuition to put yourself in their shoes and see the world from their perspective.

Organizationally savvy

You can gain further leverage by understanding how your organization actually operates, says Kelsey Miller for Harvard Business School Online (2019).

'If you're the person who knows how to get things done, go through the process correctly, get sign-off on key projects, initiatives or resource allocation, then people will naturally want to hitch their wagon to yours.'

'Similarly, if you can tie your project back to an important strategic initiative within your business, it may be easier for you to inspire others to follow your lead, as they'll want to share in the credit of a job well done.'

Equally, it is worth choosing your moment to make your move, he says. If you're in finance, your influence will be greatest during budgeting. If you're in HR, you will hold most sway when you're the gatekeeper when a project is hiring.

Positive emotions

Emotions are highly infectious within team environment, says Carol Kinsey Goman in an article for *Forbes* (May 2017). 'In business, however, the power of emotion is often discounted. We tend to believe that people think logically and act rationally. Steeped in this belief, leaders quantify everything they can in order to present information in ways that will help team members make objective decisions.'

'We are all part of an emotional chain-reaction effect. As a leader without authority, you can influence and inspire your team by understanding that emotions drive performance. Worry, stress and fear decrease physical and mental energy and impair mental agility. Positive emotions – optimism, enthusiasm, gratitude – increase energy, learning and motivation.'

MCE models and frameworks

Three ways to influence

Within organizations, you generally have three options for influencing people. First, convincing with logic. Second, by networking and building personal relationships. Third, by becoming political and running a campaign for your stakeholders: here, you will adopt a PPR model (people, power and relationships). You will find out who matters, then work out their professional and personal priorities, before establishing the dynamics of the relationships between them. Taken together, these three options give you a structure for how to influence the decisions that are going to affect you.

Four communication styles

You will be dealing with one of the four communication styles that people generally adopt:

- **Results oriented**: those who like to get to the point of what is going to happen without worrying too much about the details.

- **People oriented**: those who like to find out what's happening with you: how is life going? how was the match yesterday?

- **Support oriented**: those whose main concern is what the impact is going to be on everyone and how the team is going to sync together.

- **Analysis oriented**: those who ask what's the structure? what are the details and facts?

Once you know what someone's dominant style is, you know what approach to take.

Five degrees of conflict

You have the choice of settling conflicts in one of five ways. At either end of the spectrum, you have competition (for those who want to win) and co-operation (for those who want to be liked and maintain a relationship). In between, you have degrees of collaboration and compromise.

It's often assumed that win-win is the best solution. However, it depends on the relative importance of the result or the relationship. Collaboration can be a waste of time, for instance, if you don't expect to have a lasting relationship. Or you might think a relationship matters too much, so you're happy to take a loss.

Persuasion

As a leader, you will be confronted by a series of such turning points and decisions that you will be aiming to turn in your favour. When winning round others to your cause, you have three main questions to ask. What will they gain, of course? Perhaps more importantly, and often overlooked, what pain will they suffer if they don't follow you? So identify their pain points and highlight what their loss could potentially be. Finally, what evidence can I give them? The more tangible you are, the more likely they are to trust you.

According to an MCE module, you have three ways to persuade them. You can appeal to the mind with reason. You can appeal to the heart with emotion, Or you can be flexible in how you adapt to your audience.

With reason

As a leader, your message must make sense logically. The right facts in the right order leading to a clear conclusion will give your audience confidence. Facts alone seldom convince, however. To breathe life into your case, you can add four elements: make an analogy, use metaphors, tell a story or express an emotion.

With emotion

When using emotion to persuade, it is about being genuine. You will be positive and enthusiastic. You will reframe negative messages into positives one. You will express empathy. So, you will greet people warmly, listen with interest and stay open to new ideas.

With flexibility

Finally, you can persuade by being flexible, understanding what your audience expects and adjusting your approach. You will gauge what matters to them, what resonates with them and why they might care. You will be alive too to the form in which they like to receive messages, as well as their right tone to adopt: strong or soft? sincere or systematic? spirited or serious?

Illustration: leading without authority at Greenpeace

For the last 50 years, Greenpeace has been a pioneer in a campaigning for a sustainable planet that can nurture life in all its forms. Recent victories include taking a lead in preserving Antarctica as a wilderness and the global ocean's treaty to protect the high seas.

Fiercely independent, it relies for its funding on three million donors, rather than any grants from government or business. As an organization, it currently employs 4000 people in 26 countries supported by 20,000 volunteers.

So in one sense we could be happy with what we have achieved, says Mads Flarup Christensen, who is currently acting as its international director, after first joining Greenpeace in the early 1990s and becoming its Nordic director in 2008.

'When a UN secretary-general starts talking your language and when so many others have adopted your campaigning style, you could say how well Greenpeace has performed, except that we are in the middle of an intensifying planetary crisis.'

'Political and corporate victories are no longer enough. We actually have to aim for a systemic shift on a scale and at a speed that is unprecedented. Our campaigns for climate and biodiversity have to shift to other dimensions.'

In the past, Greenpeace has exercised its influence through creative confrontations, public information and political campaigns. Now it is adding two extra dimensions to its campaigns: it is forming alliances with progressive industries and it is mobilising the potential for people power, whether in the form of civil disobedience or online protests.

Greenpeace has always recognised the impact of leverage. Up until ten years ago, however, it mainly relied on conducting its own campaigns and trusting they would have an impact on the wider green ecosystem. As trust in political institutions declines, it is now actively developing other alliances to make a bigger systemic difference.

'We are learning to be more trusting with partners who work differently or have other goals. As long as you have top-line alignment, it works well.'

As well as business, it is now engaging more deeply with other communities, such as labour and scientists. 'The goal here is to find what unites us and how we can co-operate, rather than argue about what divides us. Without these coalitions, we cannot change the fundamental systems we are trying to challenge.'

So how does Greenpeace go about making an impact in practice? As an organization, it is a deliberately loose federation of 26 countries, each liable for its own actions. Overall, it has an assembly, a board of directors and a management team. Activities are then pursued on the principle of 'tight, loose, tight'.

'We are tight on our mission and strategic goals. We are delegated in our campaigns,' says Christensen. 'The network can test, fail and try again. We are then tight on our tools and systems. We can't instruct the network. So it takes a special set of skills to keep it all aligned.'

Conclusion

The more flexible you are in your influencing styles, the more freedom you have, says Rajeev Aggarwal at MCE. 'Most people are limited by their own tone of voice and style of communication. So they only influence their own type of people. However, if you can adopt different styles, your influence on outcomes will grow.'

As an example to participants on his MCE courses, Aggarwal likes to point to the fictional president of the United States in the TV drama, House of Cards. Like him or loath him as a character, he is a master of managing competing interests, often from a position of temporary weakness.

So, when your authority is limited, your influence depends on your ability to adapt, to understand, to communicate and to act accordingly. How you behave determines how far you are respected.

Sources

- 'How to influence without authority in the workplace', Kelsey Miller, Harvard Business School Online, Business Insights, October 2019
- '3 Crucial Skills for Leading Without Authority', Carol Kinsey Goman, contributor, *Forbes,* May 2017

CONCLUSION

In *The New York Times* of 18 October 2023, we find an article by Jeff Colgan, professor at Brown University, entitled 'Exxon Mobil's Pioneer deal is a threat to democracy'. What is aligned with this book is his conclusion: 'there is nothing wrong with wanting to turn a greater profit, but there are more ways than one for a company as large and powerful as Exxon to do so'.

Yes, there is nothing wrong to target profit or more profit. Some companies are only about profit. Others are mainly about social impact. For many, the ultimate goal lies in between.

But to realise their goal, organizations have to choose the path. That is about their leadership. Their choice will determine how they perform. Fail to make that choice clear and their efforts as an organization will be diluted.

The twelve areas presented as a model in this book give a direction. All are required to operate, but leaders choose which drivers are best for their organizations to compete and perform.

There is no good choice and no judgment is made. Whatever focus they take, companies will achieve their goals if, and only if, they can execute on that choice throughout the company. It is about cascading down and aligning teams: that is leadership.

Let's take a last example, Ryanair, the well-known, low-cost carrier, which has become the largest airline in Europe. In 2022-23, it had 22,000 employees, €11 billion in revenue and made a profit of €1.3 billion. It also has a record for conflict in the workplace and for an abrupt style in managing complaints about check-ins or delays. Clearly, we can't describe these experiences as great for customers or employees. But Ryanair is highly profitable and an extraordinary performer. So what are its main drivers here? What is leadership at Ryanair for?

I would say that the focus is on three aspects: strategy execution (the lowest price for the customer); the effectiveness of its processes (in the form of efficiency and safety) and the inspiration that the founder, Michael O'Leary, brings to the company. Any way you look at it, it is clear that the leadership is concentrating on keeping costs low, turning them into sources of revenue where they can (such as painting advertising on the planes) and operating efficiently (putting planes in the sky, where they make a profit, not leaving them standing at the gate, where they don't). In the news and the media, Michael O'Leary is widely present to share this story. Ryanair excels at cascading those drivers to its managers and teams. Even the choice not to focus on the experience of customers or employees contributes to performance and makes life uncomfortable for their competitors.

The choice of the drivers for your leadership comes first. When leaders have identified where their best chances are to outperform, they will cascade those drivers to their teams, making sure they align with that focus and adopt the desired behaviours. That is the most difficult part. Each of the twelve areas requires different methods. In our model, a clear driver defines the expected behaviours.

After reading this book, you won't look at companies the same way: you will consider them through a new lens. What are they really focusing on? And for most of them, it is quite easy. Now, what choice do you make for your organization? What is your leadership for?

ACKNOWLEDGEMENTS

I would like first to thank Adam Jolly, professional journalist and publisher. Without him, this book would never have come to life. From the start, he was enthusiastic about the project and gave numerous useful recommendations. He conducted all the interviews that appear in the text. All my gratitude to him and for his trust.

I wanted this book to reflect the reality within companies and organizations, so it was a good opportunity to ask famous names how they do it. Warm thanks to all those who gave up their time to share their story.

Maarten Broens, chief executive of APK Group, who is passionate about the creation of smart and sustainable cities, who is structuring an oorganization that can sustain growth at 20 percent a year.

Jean-Charles Samuelian-Werve, founder of Alan Healthcare, which is not the first time he has shaken up a market. Previously, at Expliseat, he revolutionised the economy seats in planes. He is also the author of *Healthy Business*.

Mads Flarup Christensen, international executive director at Greenpeace International. Running an international NGO nowadays is more complex than ever, especially when we consider the economic interests of countries and multinationals. For years, Greenpeace has been able to build a brand, a recognised name and a reputation.

Felix Sultzberger, executive chairman of Calida Group, famous for brands such as Aubade and Lafuma, where he places a strong emphasis on empowering people to implement strategy.

Eric Domb, founder of Pairi Daiza, which is frequently recognized as the best zoo in Europe. Eric had a dream and put his efforts into sharing it as a fantastic reality.

Marianna Demiri, group talent director at Imerys, a company which has made a series of strategic changes, the last of which is investing massively in lithium and taking a key position in that market. Marianna knows what it takes to maintain a high standard of talent development to align with such strategies.

Elia Congiu, chief HR officer at MSC Cruise, who is deeply involved in aligning teams to MSC's ambitions for high growth. Despite lockdowns, MSC continues to be a high performer and is launching a new exclusive brand for cruises.

Tanja Sanders, Kurita's HR director in Europe, the Middle East and Africa, who highlights the role that diversity and inclusivity now plays in all of Kurita's initiatives.

Hanne Poppe and Patricia Verdoodt in the press department at Colruyt Group who gave us an immediately positive response to our request. Colruyt Group again demonstrates how different it is on the market and how efficient its management is.

Abdelmoula El Hadi, head of innovation excellence for EMEA/ APAC at Knauff Insulation, who immediately accepted the chance to discuss the creation of a strong culture of innovation.

Nicolas Favre, director of business development at Debiopharm, whose growth depends on the successful development of partnerships, both in scientific discovery and going to market.

Dipl. Finanzing Mariella Ponearu, senior buyer at Porsche AG: Mariella is passionate about her job and her company, as much as Porsche drivers are passionate about the brand and their car.

Such a book, so rich in concepts and practices, could have never been written without the active help of MCE senior associates. Everyday they contribute to the success of organizations all round the world by delivering workshops in leadership, management and functional skills. Highly committed, they earn glowing reviews. This book is also dedicated to all of them, even if they were not interviewed for this purpose. For those who, my special and deep thanks.

Johan Beeckmans, an expert in leadership, who has been developing and delivering highly regarded solutions for MCE for years, especially in the Middle East.

Rajeev Aggarwal who has been delighting participants at his workshop for years now. Before working with MCE, Rajeev had senior management positions for PepsiCo, Frito-Lay International and Golden Tulip Worldwide Hotels.

James Capon, who, more than 15 years ago, already saw what was happening to brands caught in the middle. James is the former president of Levi's Brand and Docker.

Olivier Courtois, executive advisor with more than 30 years international experience in leadership development. He has worked in senior positions for Korn Ferry, Franklin Covey, Levi Strauss and Krauthammer International.

Frank de Keyzer who is a specialist in innovation and innovation strategies. Before working with MCE, Frank was a general manager at Heidelberger Druckmaschinen and at Agfa.

Christian Deconinck is highly active in MCE's miniMBA and customer focus programmes. After a career in retail banking in senior posts for KBC, Citi and others, he has become a specialist in change management.

Ramesh Fatania, former vice president at Shell, is an expert in leadership and in strategy, including mergers and acquisitions, who operates at the top level with executives facing strategic and leadership challenges in their organizations.

Jann Jevons, an expert in diversity and inclusion, who has guided numerous organizations along this path. She started on the BT fast-track leadership programme for talented young women, before becoming part of BT's HR strategy team.

Anna Boyko, a contributor to the MCE Women Leadership Centre, who has a passion for people and organizational development. After a career at senior positions, notably at Veon, a NASDAQ-listed communications and technology company, she is spending her time in coaching and people development.

William Mulhern, who has more than 25 years' experience of international management in customer experience, projects and crises. He spent most of his career with Cisco at a senior level.

Frédéric Ollier held several senior positions at Sanofi Aventis. One of his last assignments was vice president and global head of business development and strategy for the Animal Health Division. Frédéric has an extensive, and passionate, expertise in strategic partnerships.

Russell Houghton has more than 25 years of global expertise in leadership and talent development. Previously, Russell was the head of global senior management development for IMI plc, a UK based FTSE 100 global engineering company.

Helena Stucky de Quay, who is a expert in training, HR and digital HR. Helena acquired her experience with several companies in the hotel industry, cruise industry and in organizations like the International Red Cross.

Alain Thys, an experience architect, author and inspiring speaker, who has influenced interactions with more than half a billion customers worldwide. One of his specialities is customer intimacy and insight.

Thank you also to Emily Kamunde, who gave me the opportunity to test the model in front of an audience. I admire all she is doing with Rise and Learn, her company in Kenya.

My thanks too to Constance Cramer, Martin Emrich, Jaime de Pinies and Elena Panizza for your confidence, help and views.

Last but not least, I would like to thank my colleagues at MCE for their advice and support. In particular, Anaïs Parfait, who built most of the graphs for the book; David Goodwin for his marketing eyes; Benedicte Steyns for her trust in the project; Vincent Danvoye for his continuous support; Dominique Wauters and Antti Kirjavainen for their active help in setting up interviews.

I am equally grateful to the many contributors and supporters who have believed in this project and strengthened my conviction in writing it.